# FACILITATING GROUPS TO DRIVE CHANGE

BETTINA BÜCHEL AND IVAN MOSS

# Facilitating Groups to Drive Change

First published 2007 by
PALGRAVE MACMILLAN
Houndmills, Basingstoke, Hampshire RG21 6XS and
175 Fifth Avenue, New York, N.Y. 10010
Companies and representatives throughout the world

PALGRAVE MACMILLAN is the global academic imprint of the Palgrave Macmillan division of St. Martin's Press, LLC and of Palgrave Macmillan Ltd. Macmillan® is a registered trademark in the United States, United Kingdom and other countries. Palgrave is a registered trademark in the European Union and other countries.

ISBN-13: 978–0–230–54929–6
ISBN-10: 0–230–54929–2

This book is printed on paper suitable for recycling and made from fully managed and sustained forest sources. Logging, pulping and manufacturing processes are expected to conform to the environmental regulations of the country of origin.

A catalogue record for this book is available from the British Library.

A catalog record for this book is available from the Library of Congress.

10  9  8  7  6  5  4  3  2  1
16  15  14  13  12  11  10  09  08  07

Printed in China

*For two important families in our lives*
The Raub family – Steffen, Julian and Aline
The Moss family – Grainne, Orla and Aoife

# CONTENTS

## APPENDIX 5

## APPENDIX 6

# LIST OF FIGURES

# LIST OF TABLES

# PREFACE

# Why write this book?

Throughout the business world, many great strategies never get implemented. Many intelligent leaders fail and many strategic initiatives cause more problems than they solve. Often that is because people refuse to change or fail to agree on the changes to be made. Many leaders of strategic initiatives know this, and know facilitation can help to build commitment to change within organizations and teams.

Most change leaders have an *instinct* for when to use facilitation. But they don't necessarily understand the underlying principles. As such, most change leaders are unsophisticated users of facilitation. They simply make some educated guesses about who to use. Then they commit almost total trust to their facilitators to design and deliver "appropriate" interventions. Some of those change leaders get lucky. But many don't. Real change inevitably involves conflict. Good facilitation can channel that conflict into productive, creative solutions and build deep commitment to change. But if managed badly, such conflict exposes and then fails to resolve tensions in teams and organizations – making change harder, not easier to achieve.

We have written this book to try to help the many intelligent, well-intentioned change leaders in the world to become more sophisticated users of facilitation. Our goal with this book is to increase their chances of success by helping them know how to use facilitation to best support change. This involves selecting and working with competent facilitators with a depth of expertise relevant to the change initiative. It also means being able to judge the real quality of a facilitator's work with a group. And to know what to do to ensure that changes agreed during facilitated processes are implemented.

We hope that this book will help you, your colleagues, and your organization to experience more success in getting people to commit to change by using facilitation appropriately. At the same time, this should result in more great strategies being implemented by supporting intelligent change leaders to survive and thrive in the risky world of building organizations fit for the future.

# ACKNOWLEDGEMENTS

We would like to thank the faculty and staff of IMD and the intelligent, challenging individuals from many cultures and organizations with whom we have had the pleasure to work and who have provided many ideas and exercises for this book. They have all in different ways greatly enriched our understanding of using facilitation to drive change.

Grainne Moss and Andrew Kilshaw have our lasting appreciation for their thoughtful contributions to the initial work which encouraged us to write this book. We also thank Vodafone (and more specifically Nick Holley) for their request to develop a first version destined for facilitators.

Caroline Taggart's insightful editing helped us greatly. And Don Antunes's background research and contribution to the annotated bibliography must be specifically acknowledged.

Many people have contributed to this book, but the responsibility for any errors or omissions lies with us. We sincerely hope there are none. But we do hope that for all readers there are within this book at least one or two opinions and ideas which will provoke debate or reflection.

Finally, we owe a big thank you to our families, who have been supportive and encouraged us in this project. We are truly grateful.

# INTRODUCTION

On 17 September 2004, Anders, head of the European construction chemical company Omnius, swallowed hard as he walked out of his session with the COO.[1] The message had been clear: construction chemicals revenues across Southern Europe were unacceptable on all measures: 22% less market share than in Northern Europe, average prices 14% lower, margins 32% lower and sliding. A credible recovery plan was needed. Soon.

Eric, his finance director, and Peter, his VP sales and marketing, were following Anders down the corridor, arguing loudly. "Hiring more salespeople and changing the bonus scheme isn't going to work," raged Peter. "The people we've got aren't lazy or stupid, Eric. We're losing business because the reliability of our deliveries and the quality of our customer service is terrible. The sales guys are discounting prices because they have to, not because they're soft on customers. It's all about sorting out our supply chain and logistics."

But Anders wasn't listening. He'd heard it all before. His job had become more difficult as the products became commodities. But if he didn't change the numbers in Southern Europe there wouldn't be any better jobs in Omnius coming his way anytime soon.

Anders stopped in front of the elevators and pushed the call button. Three lifts for a 15-storey building meant waiting. It was ridiculous. Suddenly his impatience with Eric's desire just to squeeze the business harder boiled over. "Don't be so naive, Eric," he snapped. "Peter's right. Our problem is we're not competitive. Doing more of what we've always done will get us nowhere. At best, there'll be marginal sales growth. But Peter, you're wrong too. Running a good supply chain isn't easy. We can't just point the finger at operations and walk away. They aren't lazy or stupid or doing easy jobs badly either. We have a systemic problem in Southern Europe. We need change from everyone. We need people working together, coordinating better … and soon."

Finally the lift arrived. Anders said goodbye to Eric and Peter and walked in. The doors closed. Anders' shoulders dropped. Having seen the

COO in full flow, perhaps Peter, Eric, and the rest of the team would start to accept the urgency of the problems in Southern Europe. Perhaps they would see they'd all tried the easy fixes, but that turning things around required more radical solutions.

As the elevator dropped, Anders took his cell phone from his pocket and tapped it impatiently. No signal in the lift. He needed to talk to Jürgen, a professional facilitator with whom he had had a couple of speculative meetings. Could facilitated workshops with Jürgen really build a new strategy for Southern Europe that would work? It would be a lot quicker and a lot less painful to just pay the money and get a team from Boston Consulting Group (BCG) to give them a new strategy.

Finally the lift stopped. Anders stepped out and hit dial on his cell phone. Jürgen's voicemail again. Jürgen was always busy, that's for sure. But was he any good? He needed to meet with him again. He didn't trust this guy yet – he didn't know him well enough. If Jürgen wasn't up to managing real conflict, the tensions in the team between people like Peter and Eric would boil up and boil over. But bringing in BCG would be a waste of time if the team did not accept and implement the proposed solutions. As Anders mentally rehearsed his options, he came to the conclusion that, as far as Southern Europe was concerned, only a solution agreed upon among the team would do the trick.

Anders is not alone. His situation is not uncommon. Probably you have had a similar experience, similar doubts. Anders needed a real strategy with buy-in from his team. Like you, he knew that only 30% of strategic change initiatives are fully or mostly successful.[2] And often that is because people fail to change or fail to agree on the changes to be made. Like most successful change leaders, Anders knew facilitation could help people to build commitment to change within organizations and teams.[3] But only if used correctly.

Facilitation is about engaging groups to develop a shared solution to a problem by exchanging information and beliefs in order to increase the acceptability of the developed solution to all concerned. This contrasts with training, which involves skill-building, or consulting, which is about proposing solutions to problems. The facilitated groups can either be intact management teams or a group of people from the organization brought together because their input is likely to produce a widely acceptable solution.

Like Anders, most change leaders have an instinct for when to use facilitation. But they don't necessarily understand the underlying principles. As a result, they simply make some educated guesses about who to use. Then they commit almost total trust to their facilitators to design and deliver "appropriate" interventions. If you want to be more certain about when and how to use facilitation to increase your chances of creating real and lasting change, then read on.

We worked with Anders to help him to become a more sophisticated user of facilitation – to know what questions to ask Jürgen; to know how to judge the quality of Jürgen's work; to know what he, Anders, needed to do to ensure that the decisions the group reached with Jürgen were implemented in the business. It didn't take long, but it did make a big difference. This book can do the same for you.

Like Anders, if you become a sophisticated user of facilitation, your chances of success in getting people to commit to change will grow. You will be able to choose facilitators confidently and make judgments about when and how to use facilitation to support your change initiatives.

Effective facilitation interventions can help groups to work together more effectively through the process of challenging and changing their shared values and beliefs – their "mental models." When this occurs, groups build new shared values and beliefs that are both more deeply "shared" within the group and help them to perform better. Groups must begin to see situations, problems, and opportunities from new perspectives, interpret them differently, and so change how they act in response to those issues. While individual changes in beliefs are difficult to achieve, changes in collective beliefs are even more pervasive. This is because collective beliefs ("shared mental models") are embedded in routines and organizational practices that are learned over time. They are socially legitimized and act as barriers to change.

Organizational change is often a difficult process for those affected and often unsuccessful. To ensure change, individuals and groups have to revisit the values and beliefs that have guided their decision-making and actions, and develop new ideas about what is important and how issues are interrelated. In consequence, the potential for conflict and lack of objectivity is high – both from those proactively seeking to create change and those who they want to change with them. When conflict and lack of objectivity occur, groups are more likely to work inefficiently and to a suboptimal outcome.

Anyone who pretends this is simple is either patronizing you or underestimates the difficulty of the task. Equally, anyone who cannot explain to you how to work with such groups lacks an understanding of the principles needed to navigate successfully through facilitation, and is likely to fail.

## Facilitation requires skilled and competent facilitators who understand the fundamental principles

Skilled and competent facilitators not only support the meeting process but must also be actively involved before and after events.

In part, the facilitation process is one of creating structure. The facilitator and change leader create boundaries which stop groups from descending into unproductive conflict and ineffective behaviors when working together.

The facilitation process is also very dependent on the facilitator's skill. Productive outcomes from events depend on the ability of individual facilitators to manage relationships with and within the group. And as all salespeople know, great relationships are the product of three things – preparation, interaction, and follow-up.

Strong facilitators enable the group to reflect more deeply on more complex issues by maintaining group effectiveness and engagement in the face of conflict, uncertainty, and complexity. This book shows you how to ensure that the facilitators you hire are capable of doing that and how to support them in that difficult task.

## Any facilitation event is a three-stage process – planning, delivery, and post-event follow-up

Figure 1.1 (in Section 1) outlines the key elements of the design and delivery of successful facilitation events. These issues also form the core structure of this book, defining:

- What is required in *planning* a facilitation event so that it has the potential to create momentum for change.
- The key elements in *guiding* a facilitation event effectively – and so creating momentum for change.
- What is required for *follow-up* and *implementation* after an event to develop an implementation road map and to get buy-in from a larger group of stakeholders.

While we focus on specific facilitation events in this book, it is worth noting that getting buy-in to change frequently requires a number of facilitated events over a longer period of time.

## How to use this book

This book outlines a pragmatic approach to selecting the right facilitator and then to ensuring that the facilitator engages effectively with stakeholders and the team to develop a shared view of what needs to be done.

*Section 1 clarifies the key concepts and principles underpinning effective facilitation.* In doing so, it explains what effective facilitation achieves and how, in order to produce change. Importantly, it shows how mental models guide and coordinate the actions of groups and organizations – and that to create lasting changes in organizational behavior, it is necessary to change those underlying shared beliefs.

To create change, facilitation uses two essential processes: *framing* – considering alternative "frames" or interpretations of situations; and *conflict engagement* – challenging existing mental models and developing new shared mental models within the group. In this context, conflict can be positive, even essential, necessary if a group is to take a fresh angle on a problem. Framing and conflict engagement are used to encourage groups to go through the processes of *inquiry* (exploring new ideas) and *advocacy* (proposing new interpretations of situations) and explore differences in values, beliefs, and behaviors. Facilitation helps groups to work through these processes more effectively – by carefully selecting the most appropriate tools and techniques and then applying them skilfully.

*Section 2 explains what must be done **before** facilitation events* to create the potential for successful change. In particular, it shows how to select an appropriate facilitator, how good facilitation event design and planning relies upon the need to develop shared mental models, and how, in practice, activities can be consciously designed into facilitation event agendas to create shared models within the group.

When planning an event, it is essential for the facilitator to diagnose the organizational context of the change initiative and problems to be worked on by the group – plus the group structure and what the group requires to work effectively on the task. Doing this enables the facilitation event to be relevant to the group, the organization, and the task – and so increases the chance that its solution will be relevant and feasible for the organization.

*Section 3 explains what must be done **during** facilitation events* to create momentum for change. It shows how facilitators can consciously use framing and conflict engagement to move groups toward change, to maintain group effectiveness, and so create better solutions. The key challenge is to ensure that this conflict is productive, helping the group work toward new insights and solutions.

*Section 4 explains what must be done **after** facilitation events* to ensure that change occurs and is implemented and embedded. It shows what facilitators and leaders must do to maintain the momentum for change and ensure that decisions are translated into action.

Follow-up after an event is all about turning recommendations and decisions into a real, measurable outcome and to know what to do to ensure that changes resulting from facilitation are implemented. Here, the core disciplines of implementation and the task of gaining adequate support from stakeholders to enable implementation are key.

## Book overview

In this book, we offer guidance on what key activities must be completed at the planning, guiding, and post-event stages of facilitation. In addition, we provide research findings, a competency assessment questionnaire for facilitators, an annotated bibliography for the interested reader on the topic, facilitation examples for a wide range of interventions, practical information for the set-up of a facilitation event, and a checklist for change leaders.

- The *research findings* summarize the empirical work we conducted which led to this book.
- The *facilitator competency assessment questionnaire* furnishes an analysis of skills that the facilitator will need to run a successful event and will help you to select the right facilitator for your team and your change initiative.
- The *annotated bibliography* provides abstracts and references of easily readable articles on individuals, groups and organizations and their role during the planning, delivery and post-event stages of facilitation.
- *Sample exercises* illustrate the principles and ideas we explain, to show how facilitators can use frameworks and tools to help groups to engage in productive conflict and debate, and to share a small selection of the tools we use and frequently find effective.
- The *practical information* helps to set up a facilitation event by offering checklists and guidance on issues of logistics.
- *Checklists* are provided to change leaders to assure themselves that their facilitation events will be adequately planned, delivered and followed up.

Facilitation can provide a key route to creating buy-in of the need for change and for subsequent change initiatives. But this only happens when it is done in the right way and in the right circumstances. We therefore believe that every change leader and every facilitator needs to understand the guiding principles of facilitation.

This book will make the principles of effective facilitation explicit for you – increasing the probability of success of your change initiative

# SECTION 1

## Facilitation – How it works

# Introduction

To use facilitation, it is important to have a sound understanding of the theoretical foundations of facilitating groups. When your washing machine is broken, you probably call on a technician to help. You may have ideas about why the machine isn't working, but you don't really know where to start mending it. When the technician arrives and conducts a diagnostic test, he or she knows how to fix the problem. The technician has a mental model of the way the various parts of the machine interact and this model helps him or her to intervene and repair. Without this model, we really don't know where to start and what effect an intervention may have.

The same applies to facilitation. The purpose of this section is to clarify key concepts and principles underpinning effective facilitation. In doing so, it explains what good facilitation achieves and how, in order to produce change.

## Facilitated events help groups to change their values and beliefs

Within organizations, individuals need to coordinate their actions in order to accomplish organizational goals. To do so, they develop shared "mental models" based on common values and beliefs which become the basis for making decisions and taking action. Facilitated events are an opportunity for groups to develop shared mental models by sharing and exchanging information and beliefs ultimately leading to a course of action.

Outdated mental models restrict the ability of groups to perceive the need for change, or to reach new solutions to problems, and therefore make it difficult to achieve higher performance. Strong signals – such as a severe decline in performance, a conflict within the group or even a crisis – are frequently required before the need for change is recognized. Facilitated group interventions can be very helpful here. The result of these signals is a recognition of the need for change, which is the starting point for considering alternative courses of action.

When recently working with a European medical device management team, we found they had recognized that the UK organization was not performing – not achieving its growth targets. Their view was that the problem was due to organizational inefficiencies. As it turned out, the growth targets were unrealistic. Instead of bringing costs into line with realistic growth targets, the management team kept on adding resources in an attempt to obtain growth ambitions that were based on a false assumption: that it was possible for the UK subsidiary to grow without taking market share away from competition. They had not taken into account signs that the overall market had just started to decline.

While there are a large number of different terms used for mental models,[4] there is broad consensus that they mediate between individual actions and external stimuli and are particularly important as mediators in cases of change.

Figure 1.1 presents the model of how facilitation works. It shows the three stages of any facilitated event: from planning to delivery to follow-up. While the focus here is on a particular event with one group of individuals, other facilitated events frequently have to occur over time in order to get the buy-in of those affected by change.

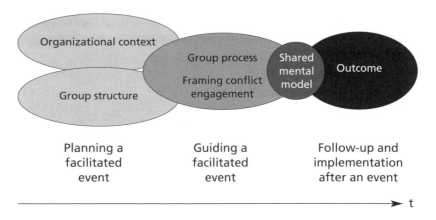

FIGURE 1.1 Facilitation model: how facilitation works to develop shared mental models

At the beginning of the facilitation process, the change leader plays the key role of choosing the facilitator and briefing him or her on the organizational and group context within which the outcome has to be achieved, but other stakeholders are also frequently involved. Therefore a deep understanding of the organizational context and its stakeholders as well as of the group is necessary. During the event itself, the facilitator plays the dominant role, enabling the sharing of different individual perspectives in order to reach a shared mental model. The responsibility for post-event follow-up lies with the change leader. We will now outline what we mean by shared mental model, group process and contextual factors.

## Throug\ roups work together to create a new mental model

Facilitat\ an opportunity for groups to develop shared mental models \ d exchanging information and beliefs, ultimately leading\ action. Facilitated change presumes commitment on the part of the group to explore alternatives and invest time and resources to engage in collective activities. At the start of any group facilitation event, group members possess different levels of experience and knowledge needed for the collective task at hand. Even if they have some experience and knowledge in common, they will not only process information differently but also have different cognitive processing schemes.

Facilitation of group interactions leads to the creation of new shared mental models by encouraging each individual in the group to share his or her point of view. This exposure will lead to the adaptation of individual models and, over time, a common understanding among the group can be reached. We refer to this common understanding as a "shared mental model."

---

### Shared mental models – a definition

The idea of shared mental models is used increasingly to describe group decision-making processes. Theorists believe that groups or teams use shared mental models to develop a common knowledge of such things as group objectives, decision-making structure, solution alternatives, information requirements, group tasks, processes and procedures, and roles and functions of other group members. From the mental model perspective we can describe group functioning in terms of group members' sharing individually held beliefs with other group members and also working collaboratively with other group members to create shared mental models. Another way to refer to shared mental models is as cognitive representations or structures of the task, situation and context that are held in common by group members. They help group members to formulate collective explanations and expectations of the task, share problem representation and orientation, facilitate communication and coordination of group activities, and develop and sustain situational awareness.[5]

---

## Shared mental models enable efficiency and coordination of action

From this definition we see that if group members working on a problem are not on the same cognitive "song sheet" with respect to the required tasks, conditions and completion success criteria, they will have difficulty in moving toward a solution. Simply stated, individuals need to develop knowledge of what the organization has been doing, why it was doing it, and how it did it, in order to develop solutions.

Researchers have suggested that shared mental models may evolve to a higher level of efficiency as the group matures and shares more experiences.[6] The literature also supports the idea that shared mental models can evolve over time through a process of progressive convergence or overlap of the models of individual group members. Groups must be able to develop a shared mental model of their task, which includes the structure of the task components, in order to reach high levels of performance. As one individual we worked with said: "Being able to share information and opinions helped us to shape our business plan. As we worked together our initial trouble of reaching a conclusion was clearly reduced and we all shared the same background information and beliefs about the next steps."

## Outdated mental models lead to problems

Reliance on shared models can, however, also lead to problems. For example, if new conditions dictate adjustments or additions to the model to accommodate the new situation, and none are made, errors can occur. If a group allows its shared mental models to become out of date for the given situation, but still relies on those models, situations of "groupthink" may take over: group members exhibit a type of complacency by becoming reliant on automated, static problem-solving mechanisms they have developed over time. This causes them to reduce their individual contributions or defer to established group problem-solving processes. Additionally, participating in highly cohesive groups may lead individuals to conform or to defer to opinions or support decisions they may not fully agree with.

While in routine situations, the existing mental model may serve the group well as it provides a recipe toward action, this is not the case in situations of a high degree of uncertainty – frequently the situations of change. In these circumstances there are no clear rules for addressing issues, and it is here that new mental models need to be acquired. Overall group effectiveness and performance depend on how well the group recognizes the complexity of its challenge and is then willing to evaluate existing models in order to modify them when necessary.

Ultimately, any facilitator needs to address two dimensions related to shared mental models: the degree of "sharedness" within the group; and the quality of the mental model in delivering a solution to a problem (Figure 1.2).

Recognizing that the existing mental model is outdated and insufficient in addressing the problem is the first step. Once the need to change has been recognized, the question becomes "how?" This is where individuals will have differences in beliefs and it becomes the role of the facilitated event to develop a high-quality shared mental model within the group.

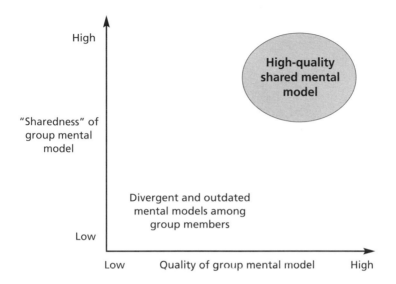

FIGURE 1.2 Influence of "sharedness" and quality on group mental models

## Group processes lead to high-quality shared mental models

During a facilitated event, groups not only need to develop shared views and beliefs, they also need to move from recognition of the need for change to the solution that will address the current situation. This means that the developed solution needs to be able to close the gap and be shared by those who develop it. For this to occur, two essential processes (Figure 1.3) must happen:

■ *Framing* – considering alternative "frames" or interpretations of the situation.
■ *Conflict engagement* – challenging existing mental models by addressing differences in values, beliefs and behaviors.

### Considering alternative "frames"

A frame is a set of assumptions and beliefs about a particular object or situation, shaped by past experiences in similar situations (or situations that seem similar in some way to those perceiving them), and it affects both how we feel and how we think. We interpret what is going on around us through a

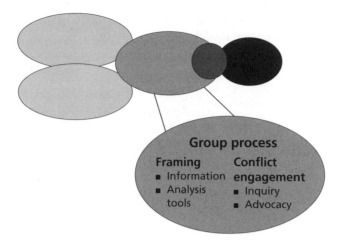

FIGURE 1.3 Group processes lead to high-quality shared mental models

lens shaped by our personal history and our current social context. Framing is therefore a process of creating meaning – either passively and unconsciously or actively and consciously – that is not a necessary or factual aspect of that situation. Framing is neither bad nor good; it is simply inevitable. The catch is that we tend to assume that our framing captures the truth, rather than presenting a subjective "map" of territory that could be mapped differently. By introducing new information or new analysis tools that may be relevant to understanding or solving the problem the group is tackling, groups engage in *inquiry* – accepting or developing new understandings – and *advocacy* – making decisions based on these new understandings.

To create a new shared mental model, a group must come to a new understanding of the problem it faces. The quality of the existing mental model is questioned. By offering frames that challenge their assumptions and beliefs about the current situation, groups attach new meaning to a situation – in terms of both how they think and how they feel about that situation. This in turn enables them to envisage and evaluate their existing mental model and come to the conclusion that it may be outdated. To do this, groups must either accept and interpret new information or revise their interpretation of previously held information by analyzing it in a new way.

If a group member observes an action or receives information that does not fit his or her expectations according to the initially perceived mental model of the group, he or she can generate a feedback response based on that model. Talking recently to a group exploring the option of entering the East European markets, we noticed that they believed that the decision to enter any one of these markets could be assessed based solely on the country context – political risk, economic conditions, regulatory environment. When someone from within the company (but outside the facilitated group) challenged this assumption by pointing out the importance of the existing presence and likely future expansion of competitors, the group revisited their priority listing of countries to enter. External feedback thus led to a revision of the mental model within the group. Because the group shares the model, the members can more quickly recognize any inconsistency and then identify and correct errors. When group members monitor performance, both group and individual, and provide feedback to other group members, such feedback facilitates corrections and improvements that, in turn, improve performance.

## Productive conflict must occur

In order to come to a new understanding of the problem and create a new shared mental model, the group must also challenge its existing frames, create new frames, and make decisions. All these steps involve conflict. *Conflict engagement* in this context refers to a process of social interaction among a group of people involving a struggle over claims to resources, information, beliefs, and other preferences and desires. Researchers have suggested that conflict exists where real or perceived differences arise in specific circumstances and engender emotion as a consequence. While the potential sources of conflict are almost infinite, it is a natural phenomenon in social interactions, as natural as harmony. In most cases, goals can't be reached without some form of conflict.

Productive conflict will ensure that the group develops a sense of cohesion, the emergence of creative ideas, the formulation of new services, and increased enthusiasm and purpose. Functional outcomes arise as group members examine, compare and reconcile differences of values, beliefs, and behaviors. This type of conflict engagement leads to high-quality shared solutions and effectiveness as the energy of the group is focused on group activities. Conflict due to differences in mental models can help the group reach a consensus by sharing different perspectives.[7] Through communication, alternatives are developed, innovative thinking is enabled, and decisions are more likely to be accepted by the group. In these circumstances, underlying assumptions of problems are not taken for granted and group members can speak their mind. Once consensus has been reached, group decisions are easier to implement.

## Influence of contextual factors

While framing and productive conflict can help lead to shared mental models, there are also contextual starting conditions that need to be understood in order to develop an effective facilitation outcome. The two most important are the organizational context and the group participants of an event.

Given that the results of the facilitated group event will impact the organization, rather than just the individuals involved in the event, it is important to understand the context within which this will happen. If the solution developed by a group is not acceptable to key stakeholders, then the outcome has a limited chance of leading to action. Therefore, the change leader and the facilitator need to understand the different perspectives of the problem on which the group will be working in the context of the existing organization.

Understanding the group and its participants is equally important as this has an influence on potential conflict within the group and therefore on the expected speed of reaching a shared mental model. The likelihood of a solution developed by a facilitated group being implemented also depends on including the "right" stakeholders in the group to start with. Again, change leaders and facilitators need to be aware of the group composition, as this impacts the outcome of any facilitated event.

### Understanding the organizational context

Understanding the organizational context involves knowledge about the vision and mission of the organization, its structure, processes, culture, and rewards. Key questions emerge that need to be understood by any facilitator:

- Is the vision and mission of the organization shared – particularly by the group participating in the event?
- How is the organization structured? What are the power relationships within the organization?

**An example of how to understand the organizational structure**
A facilitator presented the following situation as an illustration of how he works to understand the organizational structure: consider having participants graphically sketch out on a flip chart where their group sits in their organizational structure. I use blue and red lines to indicate interdepartmental relationships that are either strong or eroded. In the same way, I ask the group to draw different-sized circles to indicate the degree of influence that each department has on the group's performance. Finally, I ask them to indicate any impending changes to their organizational structure, as a result of such factors as departmental reorganizations and reductions to staff. This helps to understand the context that the group faces post-event.

In addition, the following questions are useful to understand:

■ What processes help to enable coordination within the organization?

■ What are the values and beliefs that organizational members generally share and that guide their behavior?

■ On what basis are people rewarded for their work?

■ Are there any problems with the organization set-up and have these been addressed previously? Successfully?

Answers to these questions will allow an assessment of factors that can contribute to a group being effective. It will also allow an assessment of whether the organizational context hinders the efficacy of the group. Figure 1.4 shows the key factors influencing the facilitation outcome.

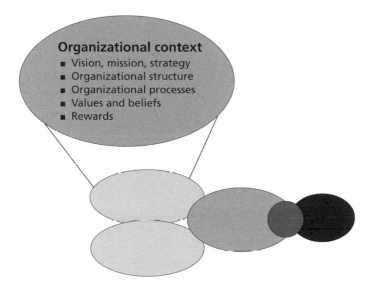

FIGURE 1.4 Organizational context affects group effectiveness

The change leader plays a vital role in ensuring that the facilitator understands the organizational context. However, while the change leader is the starting point for such a conversation, multiple perspectives are frequently needed in order to get a complete picture.

### Understanding group structure

Group structure refers to the characteristics of the group that lead to behaviors. Elements of this structure include the goals, tasks, roles, membership, norms, and leadership (Figure 1.5). A number of questions (which we will detail in Section 2) can help the facilitator to gather data about the group, thereby enabling him or her to paint a picture of its structure and assess its ability and speed to reach a shared mental model.

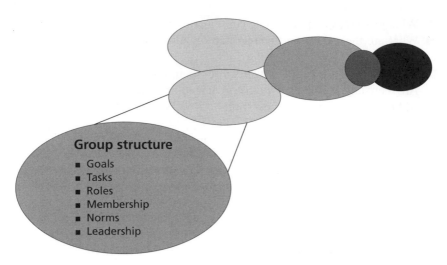

**Group structure**

- Goals
- Tasks
- Roles
- Membership
- Norms
- Leadership

FIGURE 1.5 **Group structure affects group effectiveness**

It is important to collect the data from different sources of input, because what is being constructed is a puzzle that might consist of multiple "group realities." Limited information sources (interviewing only the group leader) and restricted viewpoints can lead to a skewed perspective, like painting a picture while wearing dark sunglasses. The change leader will have to provide the facilitator with access to people in order for her or him to develop their own picture.

Here is a set of key questions that need to be answered and which we will revisit in Section 2:

- Is this group an intact team or a group of individuals working together?
- Does this group have a leader or is it self-led?
- Are all group members equal?
- Is the group diverse or culturally homogeneous?
- Has the group established explicit norms?

**Group assessment**

We recently worked with a team from the food industry who had the assignment to look at the competitive advantage of a part of their business. The individuals in the group were all seen as high potentials, although some were more senior than others. They came from different functions and international locations, did not work together on a regular basis, and no leader had been assigned ahead of time. Therefore there were no norms they could refer back to. As a result, they not only struggled with developing a solution to the assignment but also with conflicts among themselves. At the end of a five-day event, one of them said: "If we had not had a facilitator, we would not have come through our crisis. Given our different perspectives to start off with, it took us longer to reach a shared point of view."

## Group facilitation is a powerful means to engage a group to improve performance – when used appropriately

Ultimately, group facilitation is a powerful means to engage a group to improve performance, but like any other method, it has its limitations. Facilitators can intervene in the group process and structure to improve performance only if the group has the authority to implement the changes it proposes and if the participants are willing to change.

Authority is necessary because the outcome needs to be acceptable to other stakeholders within the organization, and if the organization is unwilling to accept the outcome, the change leader, the facilitator, and the group all face an uphill struggle. If a group is unwilling to change because of a perceived lack of choice, comfort level or other factors, facilitation may also be unsuccessful.

The readiness of the organization to accept the solution developed by the facilitated group is an important determinant of implementation success. Without this readiness, change leaders and those whose responsibility it is to implement the change face a great challenge in getting the organization to understand and support the new solution. It is in these cases that leaders may want to ask facilitators to help them create a sense of urgency, by getting individuals to accept the fact that they have outdated mental models and then developing shared mental models and a commitment to change among a key group of stakeholders. In the next sections, we will explore the specific steps that need to be done to plan, deliver, and follow-up on facilitation events for them to be effective.

# SECTION 2

## Planning a facilitation event

# Introduction

We have proposed a model of how successful facilitation is dependent upon successful completion of three key steps – event *planning*, *guiding* an event, and post-event *follow-up* and *implementation*.

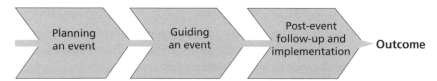

In this section we detail what is required to *plan* and *design* a facilitation event so that it has the *potential* to create momentum for change. In most cases, the change leader will have a first idea of the objectives associated with the change journey and this is normally the starting point for planning an event. These objectives then need to be refined in order to develop an agenda with the facilitator. Doing this requires:

- *Choosing an appropriate facilitator:* Using an effective selection process.
- *Establishing an effective change leader–facilitator relationship:* Agreeing the roles, responsibilities and mutual expectations of the facilitator and change leader.
- *Understanding the organizational context:* Conducting a needs analysis and engaging with stakeholders.
- *Selecting and understanding the group:* Selecting a group appropriate to the issues identified is essential. Then, to be able to help the group to work effectively, you must understand its stage of development in working together, the organizational context it works within, and so what constitutes group effectiveness within that context.
- *Designing the event agenda:* Selecting and sequencing relevant activities and inputs to support the group as it works toward the event objectives.
- *Pre-event communication:* Managing group and other stakeholder expectations of the facilitation process.

As a change leader, how long you spend planning a facilitation event will always reflect three things: the length of the event; the complexity of the problem; and the importance of the changes likely to result.

Planning a one-day facilitation event to update a procurement team's annual plan and project allocations, we would jump through these planning stages very fast – a draft agenda might be agreed within a day, and the event design finalized after one or two further meetings.

Planning a week-long intervention with a company board to develop a five-year strategy to cope with changing consumer preferences would take a lot longer. A lead time of several months would be common.

## Selecting and working with a facilitator

A facilitator's competence in planning, designing, and executing a facilitated process will have a direct impact on the quality of the decisions made and the probability of any changes having a lasting effect.

So the change leader's first criterion in selecting a facilitator should be to ensure that he or she brings a foundation of relevant experience and skills to work on the group task. Then, once a facilitator has been engaged, a needs analysis (which we shall explore later in the chapter) enables the objectives and requirements of the facilitation process and the facilitator input to be more clearly defined. The competencies required to support the group in its task become clearer. Using this increased clarity, both the change leader and the facilitator should periodically review the appropriateness of the facilitator to continue to work with the group.

### Recommended processes for choosing facilitators

> **Wherever possible, make an initial choice between facilitators based on their capability to deliver lasting momentum for change – in the group and in the organization.**

Within reasonable limits, the best approach is to separate entirely the issues of suitability and cost. Typically, differences in cost between individual facilitators are tiny compared to the potential financial impact of lasting change. While you may not be able entirely to ignore the issue of short-term cost, if, as a change leader, you are overly cost-focused, it does raise the question of how important the change initiative is and how committed the organization is to it.

#### *Choose carefully when change is complex and important – regardless of the length of the facilitation event*
As a change leader, you will be tempted to choose a facilitator more carefully

for longer interventions and more quickly for shorter interventions. But short interventions can sometimes be more important in terms of impact on the organization and can attempt to resolve more complex issues. For example, changes to the sales force bonus system might be debated and decided in less than one afternoon. Decisions like these are often made in relatively informal meetings, with little prior planning, limited stakeholder engagement, and no formal facilitation. Yet these are important decisions that affect the incentives and performance of the whole organization.

As such, the amount of care you devote to choosing the right facilitator should be based more on how complex and important the group task is, and less on the length or cost of the facilitation event.

### Assess the relative skills of possible facilitators

When choosing a facilitator, look carefully to ensure their past experience has equipped them to meet your needs. You must consider their competence to run events with your people, within your organizational context, and within the boundaries of your objectives.

In making this choice, you must inevitably rely heavily on your own judgment, supported by informal evidence through references and recommendations from your network. It can be a difficult task, but it is always worth spending time and thought finding the right person for the job.

A facilitator's competence to work with the group and organization on a specific task depends on three things:

1. *Does the facilitator have enough experience and sufficient knowledge of the subject area to be able to select and use analysis tools appropriate to the group task?*
   For example, a facilitator who has worked exclusively in manufacturing process redesign for many years might lack the tools and experience to assist a group working to predict future changes in consumer preferences.

2. *Does the facilitator have the skills and experience to manage the type of conflict within the group and with stakeholders that the change initiative will create?*
   For example, a facilitator who has focused on helping IT project teams to work through conflict about how to make a new technology work may struggle to help a group developing a hospital budget – where conflict is based more on value differences ("heart surgery matters more than mental healthcare").

3. *Does the facilitator have the skills and experience to design and guide a facilitation process appropriate to the complexity of the group task?*
   For example, a facilitator skilled in short, half-day interventions to help

groups rapidly prototype solutions to specific problems may struggle to manage a project to develop a new business unit strategy using a sequence of interventions over three months.

Evidence-based questioning techniques – asking for real past examples of situations encountered – will give you good insight into the experience and style of prospective facilitators.

The questions you ask and competencies you test should also reflect the particular skills that are important to the intervention and the wider change process. To do this, consider the depth of facilitator input required in planning an intervention, guiding events, and post-event follow-up.

For example, a facilitator working with a business over the course of a year to help it develop a strategy for entering the bottled water market in Eastern Europe would need a broad and deep range of analysis tools to select from that could aid the group in its work – ranging from growth strategy models to tools for diagnosing organizational culture and designing organizational change initiatives. On the other hand, a facilitator aiding a group to develop health and safety procedures for a new piece of complex machinery would require command of a different and perhaps smaller set of tools and facilitation techniques – but with a need for competence in using risk assessment techniques which wouldn't have been necessary in the previous example.

Good facilitators will be able to articulate their particular skills and limitations and so be more able to objectively fulfil their responsibility to assess their own suitability for an assignment and competence to work with an organization on a particular issue. Facilitators also need that self-understanding in order to identify how to develop their professional competence.

Our model of facilitator competency and the accompanying questionnaire, explained more fully in Appendix 2, are designed to help you as a change leader to evaluate in more detail the competencies of facilitators when selecting them and later when evaluating their performance.

It can be used in two ways:

■ If you have already worked with a facilitator, then you, the change leader, can complete the questionnaire yourself.
■ If you have not worked with the facilitator before, you can ask him or her to complete it and then use it to guide a discussion with them to explore their "fit" for the task at hand.

Before entering into such detailed evaluation of facilitators, a preliminary assessment of their potential capability is often useful. The questions in Table 2.1 are helpful in making this first assessment.

TABLE 2.1  Questions to ask facilitators – guidance and examples

**Designing and planning events**
- When have you succeeded in designing an event that has enabled a group to work on detailed tasks while maintaining a clear perspective of the wider context of the task?
- In what situations have you designed events where as facilitator you took a proactive, directive role with groups and why? In what situations have you planned an agenda to give a group strong autonomy and why?
- When have you not accepted to act as facilitator for a group or a particular change process and why?

**Guiding facilitation events**
- In what situations have you succeeded in remaining independent and objective when working with a group, despite having formed strong opinions of your own or encountering values and behaviors that you do not personally support?
- When have you faced real problems getting a group to draw conclusions, make decisions and commit to recommendations and further action? What did you do to overcome these obstacles?
- When have you faced difficult conflict within a facilitated group, and how did you handle it?
- When have you faced strong hostility to your role as a facilitator, and how did you handle it?
- When have you faced an unmotivated group, uninterested in their task and/or demotivated and/or lacking energy? What strategies have you used to create momentum?

**Post-event follow-up and implementation**
- When have you created real momentum for change from a facilitation event? What were the key factors in that success?
- Have you evaluated previous events and facilitator interventions to recommend key issues to consider in designing future events?
- Have you made post-event assessments of how adequately the event design represented stakeholder interests and the organizational context?
- Have you evaluated events and facilitator interventions to recommend future development issues for both participants and facilitators?

## Determine whether to use an internal or external facilitator

An *internal* facilitator (someone from within your organization, and often not a full-time professional facilitator) is better when:

■ Good knowledge of the group members, other people in the organization and organizational culture is important.
■ Detailed understanding of business processes and technical issues is important.
■ "Transaction costs" of planning and managing the facilitation process need to be kept low (both financial costs and the organization of the event).
■ You consider that these benefits outweigh the risks of the internal facilitator having less independence and more preconceptions about the issues at hand (and of the group having preconceptions and influence over the internal facilitator).

An *external* facilitator (independent of the organization, engaged only to work temporarily with the group) is better when:

■ The facilitator's autonomy is very important, enabling him or her to be seen as totally neutral and unbiased.
■ Providing a challenge to the organization's thinking is important. External facilitators can more freely ask probing questions such as: "Why can't you ...?"
■ There is an inequality of status, power and position (or verbosity) among participants and an independent facilitator can be stronger in ensuring all group members' contributions are heard and considered equally.
■ You consider that these benefits are more important than the risks of the external facilitator having less knowledge and understanding of the people, culture, business, and technical issues involved.

Whether choosing an internal or external facilitator, you, as change leader, must also consider "transaction risk." Transaction risk is the degree of uncertainty about whether the "transaction" (that is, relationship) between the facilitator and the change leader will work out. Pre-existing and ongoing working relationships between the change leader and facilitator can reduce transaction risk. There is less risk of confusion or misunderstandings about objectives and expectations. But equally, such ongoing relationships can also reduce the facilitator's objectivity and autonomy.

**Selecting external facilitators can be used to signal greater openness to new solutions**

Recently we were engaged by a government agency providing assistance to high-growth small businesses to facilitate the development of the agency's own learning and knowledge management strategy. The CEO acknowledged that the organization's knowledge was driven by a small number of

internal experts. So he engaged an external facilitator with relevant experience to ensure that a wider perspective of possible learning strategies was
considered. This signaled that the research interests of internal experts would
not be allowed to overwhelm objective assessment of the true needs of the
organization.

One final issue you might consider is professional accreditation. Various
professional bodies provide accreditation of facilitators, including the International Association of Facilitators (www.iaf-world.org) and many national
bodies for managers including HR managers.

### Negotiating facilitator fees and resources

*For external facilitators* be realistic about the fee to be paid. In many cases,
costs reflect the facilitator's expertise, preparation time and value to you. If
you negotiate fees too far down, the facilitator will probably do less preparation and/or have less commitment to getting your organization an optimal
outcome – an expensive "win" on your part. Providing internal support to an
external facilitator can often give a basis for reducing fees without diluting
the quality of facilitation you receive.

*For internal facilitators* the key issues are typically time and support. If
your assignment adds to the existing full workload of an internal facilitator,
they will simply be unable to do adequate preparation. Investigate their
actual availability. Be realistic in your expectations of them. Respect and use
their time efficiently. Provide incentives and assistance. All are important in
getting to a change owned by the group.

### Selecting co-facilitators

Facilitation events that run with more than one facilitator are relatively
unusual. However, co-facilitation can be effective when:

- The group is big and a large number of subgroups will be formed. Co-
facilitators can ensure that all subgroups receive support and attention.
- The overall facilitation program is long, running over several days. Co-
facilitators will have sufficient downtime to maintain their personal
energy – and regular changes of facilitator can also help to maintain
group energy levels.
- You wish to balance the internal knowledge and understanding of the
organization and people of an internal facilitator with the greater independence and objectivity of an external facilitator.
- The co-facilitators have complementary styles or skills and work well
together. (However, do not assume co-facilitators will always work well

together!) For example, co-facilitators can more easily use good cop/bad cop approaches to challenge and support the group.

When selecting co-facilitators, wherever possible change leaders should select and appoint a "lead" facilitator first, then involve the lead facilitator in the selection of co-facilitators. This reduces the risk of role conflict between facilitators (competing for authority or status) and improves the likelihood of their being compatible.

## Establishing the facilitator–change leader relationship

To work together effectively to support the facilitation process, the leader of the change process and the facilitator must agree on their roles, responsibilities, and mutual expectations.

Then, to create momentum for change, they must together develop an understanding of how facilitation fits within the change leader's broader ambitions, strategies and initiatives for creating change within the organization. In some cases, facilitation events will lead to the creation of a strategy; at other times they will be more focused on developing plans for the implementation of an existing strategy.

### Roles and responsibilities of the change leader

The roles and responsibilities of the change leader in supporting an effective facilitation process are predictable. To support the *facilitator* in their task, the change leader needs to:

- Provide access to relevant resources, information and people.
- Manage the relationships with and expectations of stakeholders in the change process and participants in the facilitation process.
- Assist the facilitator in defining appropriate objectives and agendas for the facilitation events.
- Hold the facilitator accountable for performance.

This ultimately means that the change leader needs to assume multiple roles. He or she needs to act as a *customer* by holding the group accountable for its task, as *decision-maker* by making key decisions which are beyond the group's range of authority (or getting them made), as *resource-provider* by getting the group the people, information and support it needs to work on its task, and as *ambassador* by representing the group to wider stakeholders and promoting its change agenda.[8]

When a change leader is also a group member, some of these roles may be more difficult to assume. For instance, it is difficult to combine coaching the group, making decisions, and being a customer at the same time. However, as a general principle, we have found that the more accountable the change leader is for implementing the solution developed by the group, the more important it is that he or she should participate in the facilitation event. The extent to which this is the case needs to be clarified early on, allowing the change leader and the facilitator to develop a clear shared understanding of the leader's role within the group. Here three important principles need discussion and resolution:

■ Whether the change leader also expects to act and be treated as the group leader, or as an equal member of the group.
■ Whether the change leader will defer decision-making authority to the group, or (less ideally) retain final authority or veto over group decisions.
■ Whether decisions to adapt or evolve the agenda during the facilitation process will be made by the facilitator. If the change leader exercises influence over the facilitation process, whether publicly or privately, the independence of the facilitator and so their credibility and authority within the group is damaged – reducing their ability to build group effectiveness and guide an optimal facilitation process for the group.

## Change leaders should expect facilitators to hold them accountable to their responsibilities

Recently we worked with a group from a major credit card company, facilitating an intensive process to develop a strategy for increasing client satisfaction amongst key European retailers. The project team chosen was a cross-functional group of vice-presidents from across the group's main European markets, led by an experienced VP from London. In planning the facilitation event, we worked closely with both the change leader – the London VP – and the entire team to build a platform of data about the relevant markets and retailers.

In doing so, facilitators are:

■ Creating a process to ensure that the group has sufficient information to analyze key issues and take key decisions.

■ Establishing an expectation with the change leader, and the group, that he was responsible for ensuring access to relevant resources, information and people within the organization – and for managing the relationships with and expectations of key stakeholders.

## Roles and responsibilities of the facilitator

In simple terms, the role of the facilitator is to help groups create solutions to specific problems by designing and guiding a facilitation process relevant to the group task and the organization's needs.

In brief, the facilitator's role and responsibilities are to:

■ Define appropriate event objectives and design facilitation events, based on the input of the change leader and stakeholders.
■ Guide and deliver facilitation events with groups in line with the objectives, scope, and stakeholder agreement.
■ Assist the group and change leader in managing stakeholder relationships and expectations.
■ Support post-event implementation tasks where appropriate.
■ Maintain adequate evident autonomy – ensuring that the needs of all stakeholders are adequately represented.
■ Evaluate facilitation events and their impact with the change leader, group, and organization.

Autonomy and competency are fundamental to the fulfilment of the facilitator's responsibilities. Without these, the facilitator simply cannot fulfil their responsibilities to the change leader, event participants, and the wider organization.

## Mutual dependence and evident autonomy

A healthy change leader–facilitator relationship is characterized by both a strong degree of mutual dependence *and* a strong degree of autonomy that is evident to stakeholders. While this is superficially paradoxical, it simply means that the change leader and facilitator recognize their individual success and performance of their roles:

■ Are dependent on the support they receive from each other.
■ Require them to act with the needs of the organization in mind and remain sufficiently independent and objective in their expectations of each other.

The whole organization is the facilitator's client – not just the change leader. Overlooking this fact damages the organization's trust in the facilitation process and can destroy the momentum of the wider change initiatives that facilitated events are supporting.

As such, the change leader–facilitator relationship is two-way – both can and should act to define the terms of their relationship. So:

- If a change leader finds the facilitator is very passive and obedient, then he or she should be concerned about the facilitator's ability to produce an outcome that has not been unduly influenced by the change leader.
- Similarly, if a facilitator feels like an unequal partner in the design of the facilitation process, he or she should be concerned about having enough autonomy to produce a truly facilitated outcome and about the reception of such an outcome.

---

**The napkin – an experience of mistaken mutual expectations**

When we recently heard this story from a fellow facilitator in Sweden,[9] we found that issues of mutual expectations can arise even with experienced facilitators. Pia, the facilitator, had been called in to help facilitate a strategic workshop with little time for preparation. The focus was on reorganizing. When the facilitator and change leader met to discuss the workshop over lunch, the leader made a small drawing on a napkin to indicate the sort of hierarchical organizational structure he had in mind. Pia developed an event design for the workshop that was to take place a few days later and told the change leader that the purpose was for the participants jointly to create a solution.

On the day, the group worked hard to develop a solution and energy was high. Shortly before the end of the workshop, the change leader came to listen to their suggestions and was shocked. He basically said: This is not good enough. You are proposing six subgroups and my drawing had five. He had simply wanted to use the facilitator to arrive at a predetermined solution.

This behavior undermines the whole facilitation process: the facilitator has wasted his or her time, while the group feels manipulated and less likely to accept an outcome that was agreed ahead of time. It is therefore important for the change leader and the facilitator to agree in advance the range within which options can be developed, particularly if the change leader himself or herself is not going to participate.

---

## Defining mutual expectations

The relationship between the facilitator and the change leader is inevitably dynamic and adapts over time. How the relationship is defined at its start, however, is important in ensuring that a healthy, productive facilitation process follows. To help build this relationship and clarify your mutual expectations, there are some issues you may find useful to agree on before, during or following the needs analysis. Some are "strategic" issues, setting the boundaries and direction of the facilitator's role. Some are more "tactical" issues – but can impact heavily on facilitator–change leader effectiveness if mishandled or unresolved.

*Strategic issues to resolve*
- What priority will be given to the facilitation events by the change leader within the wider change process and organizational context?
- How will the change leader communicate his or her support for the event to the group and the wider organization?
- What does and does not constitute an acceptable outcome for the group or the change leader – in terms of both boundaries to discussion and minimum "progress" toward a solution?
- What are the parameters for finances and dates – realistic time requirements, fees and, importantly, explicit commitment to availability on proposed event dates?

*Tactical issues to resolve*
- How will the facilitator and change leader communicate and how frequently?
- How much autonomy will the facilitator have to communicate directly with participants and other stakeholders before and after events?
- When is it appropriate for the facilitator to take on the role of advocate for the group, either in negotiating changes to the scope of the group's task or in presenting the group's conclusions?
- What information, resources and stakeholder meetings will be provided by the change leader to assist the facilitator in the design and planning of events?
- Will attendance be mandatory? How far will participants be protected from interruptions to groupwork and from repercussions from group decisions?
- Who is responsible for "administrative issues" – from organizing food, accommodation and travel to communication, documentation and event materials?

To help achieve clarity in the change leader–facilitator relationship, facilitators often initiate an explicit discussion on mutual expectations. To do this, experienced facilitators may use:

- A prepared statement of their values, principles, expectations and the boundaries they plan to respect between the change leader and themselves as facilitator.
- Informal "storytelling," recounting key experiences to clearly signal to change leaders what they consider to be important issues in their relationship and where they think important boundaries lie. Often this is done by

discussing their thoughts about where and why past facilitation events have succeeded or failed – and if the change leader concurs with their conclusions this constitutes agreement.

As a change leader, you will often find facilitators ask you questions designed to help them understand your values, expectations, and previous experiences. Consciously preparing yourself for this conversation, by considering these issues ahead of time, ensures that you share your real priorities, not simply what is in the front of your mind at that particular point in time.

Sometimes the terms of a change leader–facilitator relationship are formally documented. Sometimes they are not. When using an external facilitator, formal documentation of key issues is common simply to provide clarity should any contractual disputes arise. But, like prenuptial agreements, it is often a bad sign if these are ever referred to (or are considered upfront with too much intensity).

## Understanding the organizational context to validate change objectives

Defining event objectives is the first concrete practical task a facilitator undertakes at the start of any facilitation assignment. The process of defining event objectives starts with a needs analysis. During the needs analysis, the facilitator must engage with stakeholders for the first time, and so begins the process of understanding their needs and managing their expectations. The needs analysis also enables the facilitator, change leader, and stakeholders to select group participants appropriate to the issues identified.

The facilitator must define the issues being faced, the reasons why facilitation is needed to solve those issues, and how the issues fit into the wider organizational context. The better the needs analysis, the more precisely you can tailor the event design to meet the organizational needs – and this takes time.

### Purpose of a needs analysis

The purpose of a needs analysis is to ensure that the design will lead to a shared mental model by a group of people who are able to drive change. The key issues to consider in detail are:

1. What are the problems or issues to resolve?
2. What are acceptable outcomes to the key stakeholders?

To conduct a needs analysis, facilitators should focus on analyzing answers to these questions. Concentrate on obtaining real examples, evidence, and data to support the answers.

The needs analysis then enables the facilitator to define the event agenda and select interventions and tools best suited to the group and the issues.

---

**Failing to prepare is preparing to fail: needs analysis is essential preparation work**

Another story we heard from friends involved two facilitators who were brought in by the CEO of a company to help with an intensive strategic planning process. Instead of being able to conduct in-depth interviews with the staff as an important part of their preparation, they had only a few informal chats. Once the facilitation event had started, it became clear that although the CEO was keen on change, the staff did not want to know – and they told the facilitators so. Although the group eventually agreed on a plan for change which was implemented, the facilitators did not enjoy the experience of working with a dissatisfied group who used the event as an opportunity to share their frustration. Later they found out that the management team had been aware of the staff's attitude, but had chosen not to pass on this information to the facilitators.

One of the lessons from the event was never to start an assignment without a clear assessment of the organization, interviews with key stakeholders – which in this instance would have included some of the staff – and an informed understanding of the likelihood of success given the circumstances.

---

Initial discussions with the change leader will usually identify the key people the facilitator needs to meet and engage with. Usually this will include representatives of all those directly or indirectly affected by possible change. For example, running a facilitation event recently to improve the design of seasonal ranges by a niche clothing brand, we included in our needs analysis the owners, management team, design team, in-house pattern cutters, fabric suppliers, outsourced manufacturers, buyers from key retailers, and finally end customers who bought and wore the clothes.

## Results of a needs analysis

An effective needs analysis will result in answers to the following questions:

- *Problem statement:* A clear definition of the business problem faced and its strategic and tactical context and importance within the organization.
- *Project objectives:* A definition of what constitutes a "solution" to the

problem – including if possible specific metrics, like increased market share, that need to be achieved.

■ *Project scope:* The breadth, longevity and limits of this project – what issues will and will not be covered.

■ *Group and group roles:* Who should participate in facilitation events and what their role and contribution are expected to be.

■ *Resources:* The financial and personal resources necessary to make the project successful.

■ *Issues, challenges and risks:* Known issues which cause or relate to the problem. This includes competing priorities, apparent technical limitations, resource constraints, irresolvable uncertainties, time pressures, and uncontrollable factors.

■ *Economic justification:* The estimated cost–benefit of solving the problem. Benefits can be quantified in terms of increased revenues, reduced costs or more efficient use of assets.

■ *Timelines and milestones:* The date by which the facilitation events must be completed to support the wider change initiatives and align with other organizational activities (for example annual budget cycles).

A good needs analysis is iterative – conversations lead to further conversations. Rather than only being guided by the change leader on which stake holders should be consulted during the needs analysis, the facilitator should allow all stakeholders to have a voice about who should contribute. The difficulty for the facilitator, of course, is to judge when they have engaged with "enough" stakeholders and collected "enough" understanding of the organization and issues. The "80:20 rule" – that 20% of the effort will often achieve 80% of the results – is an appropriate principle for facilitators to adopt, as they need to discover only what issues exist, not to become experts in those issues.

## Identifying and engaging with key stakeholders

To ensure that the objectives of the facilitation event are in line with those of stakeholders, an event should address the needs of three groups: the group participants, the change leader, and other affected parties within the organization (for whom some individual participants may be acting as representatives). We will discuss the group participants in the next section.

To effectively address the needs of the other affected parties, the facilitator has to:

■ Manage the expectations of all stakeholders about both how the facilitation process will work and the possible outcomes – as defined by the scope and objectives of the event.

■ Obtain all relevant information for the group to work with – and build acceptance with stakeholders that where uncertainty exists, the group should make decisions about how best to move forward based on existing knowledge and circumstances.

Meeting with participants and other stakeholders informally or formally during the needs analysis and design phases of facilitation planning is a good investment of time whenever it is possible. Importantly, the facilitator gains a more independent understanding of the problems and issues, plus a fuller picture of what constitutes an acceptable outcome to the stakeholders.

When conducting a stakeholder analysis, the facilitator should ask about the wider context of why and how problems occur. Issues from strategy and organizational structure, to working processes and information systems, to culture and personality all produce or reinforce problems. The role of the facilitator is to ensure that the group can produce realistic outcomes.

Equally, spending time in the organization can help to attune the facilitator to the behavior and culture surrounding the group. This increases the probability of the facilitator choosing a style of interaction with the group that builds rapport quickly.

TABLE 2.2 **Engaging with stakeholders – some key questions to ask**

■ Why is the project needed?
■ What problem does it resolve?
■ What is the background or context to this problem?
■ How did the problem arise?
■ Why does this problem matter? Particularly, why does it matter to customers, shareholders or regulators (legal, environmental and social requirements)?
■ How does the problem relate to the business strategy?
■ Who are the main stakeholders involved and how do they see the problem?
■ Is there any information or analysis needed before potential solutions can be envisaged or evaluated?

After conducting a needs analysis which may lead to the renegotiation of objectives and expectations, two situations may arise:

1. The change leader may have to accept a redefinition of the objectives.
2. The change leader may be invited to participate in the facilitation event – either as a full participant or by scheduling a "change leader briefing" slot

for the group to present and discuss their interim insights on the issues before moving ahead to develop conclusions and proposed actions.

### Lack of independence and false openness

Two issues which often question the appropriateness of facilitated events after a needs analysis are:

- *Insufficient independence* between facilitator and change leader – because of their professional and/or financial relationship.
- *False openness in change leaders* – apparent openness to a facilitated group solution masking more limited views on what outcomes they will accept.

Both issues are difficult for facilitators and change leaders to identify because of their own inevitable lack of objectivity. However, they can be deeply harmful to the change initiative if they lead to the group feeling "duped."

Often other internal stakeholders, especially those with most to lose from badly designed change, are the most reliable analysts of these risks during the needs analysis process.

When we worked with a group specializing in baby foods to redesign their product development processes, the country-level marketing groups we met during the needs analysis repeatedly pointed out that the product development teams were unwilling to spend time with them to develop a deeper understanding of regional differences in what baby foods consumers bought and why. As a result of this information, we paid careful attention during the event to ensure that the role of market information in product development was discussed in real depth.

### Needs analysis, not consulting assignment

Often facilitators will have some prior knowledge and understanding of the problem to be worked on during the event. As discussed earlier, such knowledge is necessary if they are to be effective in working with the group.

However, if in conducting a needs analysis, the facilitator becomes an expert on the problem or develops strong opinions and ideas about the issues, the participants, the organization or the best solution to the problem, then he or she damages their objectivity and impartiality. This limits their ability to fully contribute to the group.

In conducting needs analysis, change leaders must watch out for facilitators becoming trapped in a solution-seeking mode.

*Review meetings with the change leader and key stakeholders* are important throughout the design process. They help create a mutual understanding and shared ownership of the desired outcomes of the event. They are
also useful for solving any problems that may be encountered and determining each party's roles and responsibilities.

This is where facilitator–change leader contracting and needs analysis
overlap. Before beginning the facilitator–change leader contracting process,
the facilitator must have some basic understanding of what the change
leader is seeking to achieve and why. Then, to maintain and develop the
relationship, the facilitator must conduct an adequate needs analysis and
negotiate an updated definition of objectives and acceptable outcomes with
the change leader.

### Post-needs analysis review: is facilitation appropriate?

After completing a needs analysis, the facilitator must also review whether
facilitation is, in fact, the most appropriate intervention to promote change.
Based on a new deeper understanding of the issues, it may be clear that
facilitation is not an appropriate tool. If so, the facilitator must recommend
this to the change leader and other stakeholders.

Sometimes facilitation is inappropriate because there is already widespread
agreement about the need for change or the preferred solution.

For example, recently we were contacted by an engineering consulting firm
who asked us to work with a major electricity generating company for them.
They believed the client had multiple internal stakeholders who disagreed
about whether or not a major power station needed an upgrade and that
this disagreement needed resolution before they started their design work.

After several meetings with the engineering consultants, the head of power
generation within the company and many other stakeholders, we recommended that the design work should start as planned. All stakeholders in
fact agreed that a major upgrade was required. The only disagreement was
about when upgraded generation capacity would be required – based on
projections for growth in power demand. And completing the design work
would enable faster movement from decision to action once the electricity
company decided its construction timetable.

Sometimes facilitation is inappropriate because the change leader has a firm
opinion of the solution to an issue and is not open to accepting a facilitated
solution developed by a group.

For example, we were recently asked by a publishing company to work with the management team of a director responsible for commissioning to improve the effectiveness with which they attracted new manuscripts. After a conversation with the team members and the team leader, it became clear that the leader did not buy into the facilitation event. He was reluctant to have an external facilitator work with his team, because he already had a fixed belief as to what the outcome should be. In these circumstances, a facilitation event would simply not have worked.

## Selecting and understanding the group

A skilled facilitator and a good needs analysis of the organizational context are only two ingredients of a successful facilitation event that will create lasting change. The other, most important ingredient is the group itself. The two key tasks are to select a group appropriate to the issues identified, and, if it is a group that has worked together before, to understand their stage of development in working together and the context in which they work.

### Selecting the group

Sometimes group selection will overlap or foreshadow the needs analysis, for example if "the group" is an existing management team calling in an external facilitator to help them work on developing a new strategy. But there should always be a review of who should participate – ensuring that those with little to add are allowed or encouraged not to participate, and that all those with important information or viewpoints are included.

In selecting groups to work together in a facilitation event, there are four basic criteria. The group must:

- Possess skills, knowledge, expertise or experience useful to the group.
- Adequately represent and understand the needs of key stakeholders and have good access to key stakeholders and resources through formal and informal networks.
- Acknowledge the task as important and be motivated to work on it.
- Have the seniority and/or credibility for their conclusions to create real momentum for change. Only honest conversations with the change leader and key stakeholders and insights into the organizational power structure (formal and informal) will establish this.

Not everyone in the group needs to be an expert or a senior player:

■ *Diversity of perspectives is essential:* Selecting a group with diverse perspectives of the organization and/or the group task ensures that there will be debate about "what is important" and what information or analysis "means." Consequently, the values, priorities, and decision criteria to be adopted by the group will also have to be actively debated and decided. Thus, diversity prompts group members to review and adapt their beliefs and create new mental models of the situation and possible solutions.

Conversely a homogeneous group will usually approach a problem or situation with a strongly shared existing mental model – limiting their impulse to consider new perspectives and so to craft new solutions. Typically, the more homogeneous a group is, the more inputs will be required to encourage it to engage in inquiry – looking at problems in new ways.

When a group is more diverse, their diversity alone will often trigger inquiry. But they will often need more help than homogeneous groups when engaging in advocacy – resolving their different opinions and making shared decisions.

■ *Non-experts can play a very useful role:* At first non-experts may seem like a heavy burden for the group but the very fact that they know nothing often pushes them to ask obvious questions that cut right to the heart of the problem. They have the ability to see issues in a fresh light and to challenge conventional thinking. When a group includes non-experts, the facilitator often needs to build in time and activities to "bring them up to speed" and create opportunities for both the change leader and the non-experts themselves to demonstrate and reinforce their value in contributing to the group.

■ *Developmental opportunities can create constructive challenge:* Working in a high-powered group could be a great development opportunity for a high-potential manager – or simply a strong contribution to the group. The intellectual horsepower of individuals is not always aligned to their organizational status.

Equally, placing more junior staff into a high-powered group can help the group to slow down and reflect more deeply on its unspoken assumptions and priorities. When senior members of a group take the time to explain their thinking as a developmental opportunity for a high-potential junior, they are prompted to articulate their reasoning more explicitly (and so open it up for evaluation).

When integrating developmental opportunities into a facilitation process, the agenda design should include time for learning and reflection to occur. For example, during the first two days with a group, we often use "micro-lectures" of five minutes or less to explain key concepts related to how adults learn and how facilitation "works." To the participants, these micro-lectures appear to occur spontaneously – during coffee breaks, in social conversation. And their exact timing is spontaneous. But we have consciously decided in advance to share those concepts. Why? Because understanding the facilitation process improves group effectiveness. And because understanding the facilitation process and adult learning will affect their capability as managers on an ongoing basis.

In some circumstances, substantial prework may be required with individuals or groups to bring them to a position where they can usefully participate in a facilitated process. Sometimes this can be because of a knowledge gap – creating a need to "educate" participants about the issue. Sometimes it can be because individuals or the group do not feel qualified or confident to take responsibility for solving the issue. Including participants in the event design process can help to address this problem.

### Learning objectives – are they part of the event objectives or not?

Sometimes group facilitation is purely goal-focused – problem solution is the name of the game. And as fast as possible. Nevertheless, in any good facilitation process groups also learn and develop their skills in problem investigation, analysis, decision-making, and conflict management.

Sometimes facilitation events explicitly include this participant development as an event objective. These can be group and individual objectives. The important issue here for a facilitator is that if such objectives are set:

■ All stakeholders need to accept that the facilitation event is a developmental process for participants, and to agree on the relative priority of the task and learning objectives.
■ Learning objectives cannot overshadow task objectives. If they become the success criteria, then a trainer not a facilitator is required.

## Understanding the group

Once a group has been selected, the facilitator must diagnose it in order to understand:

■ How the group currently interacts and works together.
■ What are the group's existing mental models of the issues to be worked on – and how far those mental models are shared or diverse and static or evolving.

In diagnosing a group, we recommend following an explicit process including the key steps outlined below.

### Understanding group structure

As discussed in Section 1, group structure refers to the characteristics of the group that influence group behavior and the potential to work together effectively. The key questions detailed below can help you determine the degree to which the group is fragmented with temporary membership, or composed of members who represent different cultural norms, with or without explicit leadership.

### Is this team intact or a group of individuals working together?

A team that is composed of permanent, full-time members is described as "intact." In many organizations, however, team activities happen in the form of project teams and task forces, composed entirely of temporary, part-time members. For these individuals, balancing the conflicting demands of their team with the daily demands of their "real" jobs can be a major challenge.

Intact teams are more likely to have permanent goals and who belongs and who does not is clearly understood by others. Intact teams are also more likely to have entrenched group norms with which they have operated for a while. Established group norms can aid group effectiveness. But equally they can limit openness to inquiry and new interpretation of issues.

Where a team is "intact", introducing information and tools to encourage inquiry will often need focus to ensure this occurs. Where a team is simply a group of individuals temporarily working together, more time and effort needs to be devoted to forming social bonds within the group, establishing individual and group ownership of the task, and managing the process of advocacy and decision-making so that they result in productive conflict engagement and shared decisions.

### Is this group or team led by one individual or by many?

While many groups may be headed by a single leader, who operates within a clear and unambiguous reporting structure, many operate within matrix environments, in which direction and authority are split between functional and divisional leaders. Sometimes, with a new group of people working together, no formal leader has even been assigned.

In the case of an existing team with a leader, tasks and roles are often clearly defined. Leadership is understood by everyone (although not always accepted) and norms have developed as a result of the particular leadership style. When a group is new and has not chosen or appointed a leader, roles need to be defined, leadership is questioned, norms have not been established. It may be that the only thing that has already been determined is the task. In these circumstances, facilitators and change leaders need to plan for more conflict around decision-making and should devote more time to establishing and reinforcing ground rules within the group.

### Are all group members equal?

The underlying assumption of many group models is that everyone is equal. While this is sometimes the case, there are also circumstances when group members represent different reporting levels, creating power dynamics that need to be explicitly recognized. While this could be very visible, it is not always the case. Many facilitators fail to consider the more subtle power relationships that are present within a group. Even if all members share the same grade levels and titles, they may represent very different levels of power and influence, due to such factors as their access to senior managers or varying levels of technical expertise.

In groups that are characterized by subtle but significant differences in power and authority, low-power members may fail to candidly disclose their concerns, due to feelings of vulnerability and the fear of retribution. In order to reach a shared group mental model, information and individual viewpoints from all involved group members need to be heard.

As a result, change leaders should highlight to facilitators where such subtle inequalities exist and facilitators should respond by actively managing group discussions to ensure that all participants voice their opinions and are listened to. This is particularly important at "moments of decision" where the group chooses between options – in terms of what issues to focus on, how to interpret key information, how to spend its time, and what recommendations to make.

### Will the change leader be in the group?

As we have seen, often change leaders choose to be participants in the facilitated group. For the facilitator and the group, this situation provides both an opportunity and a challenge:

■ Positively, the change leader can role model productive behaviors which support group effectiveness and demonstrate their commitment to champion change initiated by the group.
■ Negatively, both the change leader and the group must work hard to escape the risk of imbalance – the change leader's beliefs, inputs, and reactions to ideas and proposals being given excessive weight in group decision-making and recommendations.

### Is the group culturally diverse or homogeneous?

Facilitators may fall into the trap of assuming that their groups are homogeneous, in that members share the same values and social norms. In many cases, however, group members come from different national cultures, or radically different corporate or functional cultures. In such situations, facilitators can easily find themselves faced with group members who hold very different assumptions about how "effective groups" function, the role of the group leader, or the degree to which they feel comfortable publicly discussing sensitive issues or questioning their team leaders' ideas. Importantly, the facilitator should be careful not to impose or overweight his or her own values, norms or assumptions about how "effective groups" function.

Where such diversity exists, facilitators should ensure that there is explicit discussion within the group about what values and norms different participants carry. Importantly, this should focus on expectations and feelings about how opinions should be voiced and how decisions should be made.

### Has the group or team experienced a change recently?

With an existing group, an understanding of how it has evolved over time is helpful to facilitators planning events. A group evolves through a life cycle and each stage of the cycle has predictable transition characteristics (Figure 2.1). The facilitator who knows what to expect in these stages is better prepared to service the group members' needs and help them to deal with the situations inherent in each stage. In particular, the facilitator can often more quickly diagnose the root causes of conflict when he or she knows about the life cycle and history of the group.

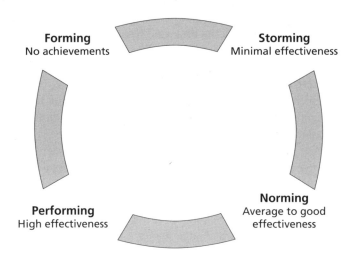

FIGURE 2.1 Group development[10]

Understanding the stage at which the group is means discovering how it has evolved over time, and the broader organizational context in which it is currently embedded. Here are three key questions:

- How has your group changed over the past year?

■ What differences would I have noticed if I had observed your group's performance over this time period?
■ How has your group got to where it is today?

These questions help the facilitator to understand the group's current level of effectiveness. Recent change is neither an obstacle nor an advantage to facilitation. It simply indicates different issues that may arise and that the facilitator needs to resolve to enable the group to tackle its task effectively.

The change leader needs to be aware of these key questions that the facilitator needs to know and help provide the information in order to help the facilitator prepare.


## Designing the agenda

After defining the event objectives, analyzing stakeholder needs, and understanding the group, the facilitator's next task is to design and plan specific facilitation events.

In essence, when establishing the facilitator–change leader relationship, conducting the needs analysis, and diagnosing the group, the facilitator answers the questions "*When* to facilitate and *why*?" This puts the event in context for all stakeholders – defining the group's scope, context, and objectives.

In designing the agenda and planning events, the facilitator answers the question "*How* best to facilitate?"

The agenda serves three practical purposes:

■ It is the facilitator's plan – how to intervene with the group to help it work effectively on its task.
■ It provides reassurance for the change leader and stakeholders – by explaining how the group will work on its task and how members' needs and concerns will be considered.
■ It provides a road map for the group – outlining the steps it will take to complete its task.


### The role of the agenda – enabling new insights

To create real momentum for change, groups must create new solutions based on new insights into the issues and problems. Thus, to support change, a facilitator must design an agenda which challenges group members to revise their beliefs about the problem, task or situation.

As discussed in Section 1, the way a group or individual "sees" a situation is their "mental model" – their theory of how different issues relate to each other. Facilitation can help groups to move from out-of-date individual or shared mental models and help to create a new, richer, shared mental model and so envisage new solutions.

The basic tools for helping groups to revise their mental models are framing and conflict engagement (Figure 2.2).

**Framing** is the use of new information and analysis tools which may be relevant to understanding or solving the problem the group is tackling, to help members engage productively in inquiry (exploring new ideas) and advocacy (proposing particular interpretations) until they succeed in creating a shared belief in the most appropriate analysis and solution for their problem, task or situation.

New information and analysis tools can serve to:

■ Promote inquiry – helping groups to accept or develop new understandings.
■ Promote advocacy – helping groups to hear opinions and make decisions.

Importantly, framing is an effective tool for helping groups to engage in productive conflict and avoid descending into destructive conflict.

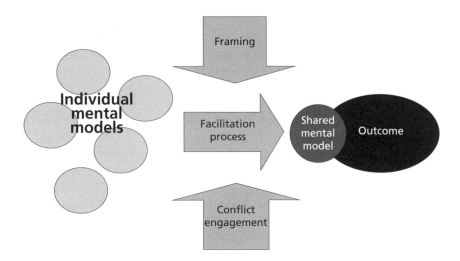

FIGURE 2.2 The role of the facilitation process in translating individual mental models into shared mental models

**Conflict engagement** means exploring differences in group values, beliefs, and behaviors in order to help the group develop new shared mental models. It is essential if inquiry and advocacy are to occur. When groups and individuals compare how they perceive issues and/or groups receive new information, conflict tends to arise. In order to develop shared beliefs, the group must engage with this conflict. The way it does this is crucial, since productive conflict allows group members to explore different interpretations of issues, values, and behaviors without substantial process losses.

### Guiding the group toward inquiry and advocacy

In planning the agenda, a competent facilitator is conscious of the underlying purpose of each activity selected within each phase of the event, and its role in helping the group to create new insights. Each agenda item should encourage the group toward either "inquiry" or "advocacy."

**Inquiry** is openness to accept and reflect on new information. Agenda items encouraging inquiry are particularly important in the earlier phases of an event. They help group members to accept the incompleteness of their existing ideas about the issues and open them up to imagine and accept new ideas and solutions.

For example, the exercise "Hall of Fame and Hall of Shame" in Appendix 4, helps group members to see how different people can hold different and often equally plausible beliefs about the causes of previous organizational successes and failures.

When we were working with the niche clothing designers mentioned earlier, this exercise highlighted a diversity of opinions about whether particular dresses had sold well because of greater attention to global fashion trends or greater attention to retailer and consumer feedback.

**Advocacy** is proposing and defending a position – an argument for a particular interpretation, decision or course of action. Agenda items encouraging advocacy are particularly important in the later phases of events. They help groups to debate and agree solutions and decisions.

For example, the "New Behaviors and Capabilities" exercise in Appendix 4 helps groups to make decisions about the priorities, tasks, and changes required to support implementation of their problem solution.

During our baby food product development project, this exercise proved useful in translating a broad intention to pay more attention to regional differences in consumer preferences into specific actions to ensure that those differences were captured and considered during new product prototyping.

## Creating the agenda

Designing an agenda is typically a two-step process. Good agenda design will explicitly separate these two steps:

■ Establishing the red thread – the sequence of key tasks the group needs to work through.

■ Selecting specific tasks, activities, and tools.

### Establishing the red thread

Before detailed event design occurs, an overview of the key tasks the group must complete and issues it must resolve is necessary. Facilitation events can vary in length from half a day to, at most, a week of continuous groupwork. Often the group will work together in bursts, with periods of days or weeks in between meetings for "other work" and to complete research, analysis or stakeholder engagement tasks. The underlying red thread of any facilitation process designed to help a group develop new shared mental models is to move from an initial focus on inquiry toward advocacy over time.

Regardless of the length of the event, the red thread of all agendas essentially consists of six major phases (Figure 2.3). The needs analysis then provides the specific key issues which must be addressed within the agenda.

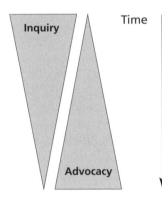

Time
■ *Opening – setting context and direction*

■ *Building a shared body of knowledge about the issues*

■ *Issue analysis*

■ *Decision-making*

■ *Implementation plans*

■ *Communication plans*

FIGURE 2.3 How the facilitation process helps a group move from inquiry toward advocacy

## A practical example of creating the red thread

Building an outline agenda for a facilitation event explicitly defines the red thread and the key tasks the group needs to complete.

In the example in Figure 2.4, we show an outline agenda we developed during the design of an intervention to help a group improve its product development strategy. It shows how we planned to move the group from inquiry through to advocacy over the course of an event.

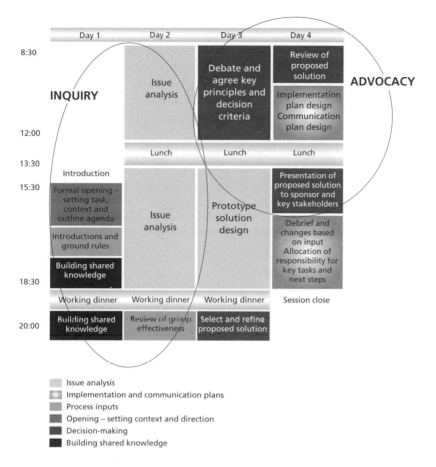

FIGURE 2.4 **Example outline agenda**

The structure of the outline agenda in Figure 2.4 above is as follows:

- *Formal opening – setting context and direction:* In order to be effective, the group must have an answer to the questions "What do we need to achieve? And why?" The event begins with an explicit statement of the task and objectives assigned to the group. This serves to help the group define its task and develop a shared understanding of the topic. Whenever possible, this opening should be given by the change leader, so that the group hears a direct view of the change leader's needs, rationale for their task, and clear expectations of their role.
- *Introductions and ground rules:* Time is dedicated for the group to discuss and establish some mutual expectations of group effectiveness.
- *Building shared knowledge:* As psychotherapists commonly say, it takes a lot of therapy before a patient is genuinely ready to enter therapy. Simil-

arly, time must be spent to ensure that all group members have an adequate and consistent understanding of the task and its context before
engaging in real "work" on the task. This includes establishing a "shared
language"– a common understanding of what is meant by what is said by
different stakeholders about the issues and what key words mean.

■ *Issue analysis:* Time is allocated to investigate the major issues facing the
group, although how best to explore those issues has not yet been
decided. As such, the facilitator is at this stage simply deciding how much
time to devote to *inquiry* and what subjects to focus that inquiry upon.
The objective in this phase of the agenda is to explore the relationships
and relative importance of different issues and build a shared agreement
within the group of how key issues interrelate.

> **Minor conflict** is predictable at this point – the group will most probably
> have diverse beliefs on the causes of those issues, and on what stakeholder
> needs should be prioritized in solving them. The goal of the facilitator is to
> *contain but not suppress this conflict* – the group needs to develop a greater
> understanding of these issues and beliefs before it has deep conflict, but
> equally will benefit from "practicing" engaging in productive conflict before
> real decision-making needs to occur.

■ *Review of group effectiveness:* Taking time to reinforce the group's effectiveness in working together is often useful – especially early in the facilitation event. Reviewing the group's progress in working together
enables reinforcement and adjustment of productive behaviors to build
the group's skills and readiness for conflict engagement. "Moments of
reflection" such as these should be both formally included in the agenda
and created spontaneously by facilitators.

■ *Decision-making:* From this point forward, negotiating agreement of
solutions and priorities within the group is the focus.

■ *Debate and agreement of key principles:* Before a group begins drawing
conclusions, making choices and recommendations from their analysis,
they must establish agreement of some decision criteria, such as feasible
implementation within a three-month period being an essential element
of any acceptable solution. In deciding their decision criteria, the group
"practice" advocacy – making decisions together, but not about the task
solution itself.

> **Major conflict** is predictable at this point – the group will have built some
> shared understanding of the issues and of different stakeholder beliefs on

"what is important." But now, advocacy must occur – decisions must be made about what stakeholder needs should be prioritized in solving the issues. The goal of the facilitator will be to ensure that this conflict occurs and the issues are deeply debated. The facilitator's skills in preventing conflict avoidance and promoting constructive conflict will be tested most here.

■ *Prototype solution design:* After having agreed some decision criteria and so prioritized stakeholder needs, the group can then move to creating prototype solutions. This is a return to a focus on inquiry – exploring ideas and possible solutions. The facilitator's focus is to hold the group back from advocacy and stop them evaluating or judging prototype solutions or recommendations too early.

■ *Selection and refinement of solutions:* Here the group moves fully into advocacy and decision-making. It is led toward building shared conclusions. Managing productive conflict is the key facilitator task – to ensure that the group comes to recommendations it can support and champion.

**Conflict** is again likely at this point – probably major conflict. For example, recently we worked with a group who earlier in the day had agreed key principles and decision criteria but found that agreement was tested when they applied those criteria. Revisiting earlier decisions is natural, normal, and predictable. Shared understanding and alignment are rarely achieved in one strike – reflection and revision are necessary and beneficial.

■ *Review of proposed solution, implementation design, and communication planning:* This is all about ensuring that the proposed changes are acceptable to the stakeholders and are therefore likely to be implemented. Advocacy – helping the group to critique and polish their conclusions and supporting logic – is the key activity.
  – *Implementation plans* define what the group and other stakeholders must do to action the decisions made.
  – *Communication plans* define how the group will influence other stakeholders to support their decisions and implementation plans.

*The success or failure of the facilitation process* is usually obvious to the group by this point. If the group has descended into **destructive conflict**, failure is obvious. If **no conflict** has occurred, failure is more implicit – the proposed solution will be built on either false consensus or inadequate investigation of the issues.

The example outline agenda shown in Figure 2.4 shows how these key phases and tasks could be sequenced for a three-and-a-half day facilitation event. In some cases, more time is required. Generally when groups have had limited experience of working together, the facilitator requires more time to reach a solution owned by the group.

### Maintaining energy and involvement – review stops and breaks

There is always a danger of trying to fit too much structured activity into the time available. Too much focus on tasks and activities leads to a "roller coaster" experience for participants and ultimately reduces the overall effectiveness of the event.

Program breaks and unstructured reflection time (whether coffee breaks, simple "time outs," meals or other unfocused activities) are an essential component of the learning cycle described above. They underline the progression through the event cycle and enable participants to digest what they have just discovered, decided or agreed to before moving on.

Equally, formal breaks for the purposes of review – confirming previous decisions and group understanding of key issues – can be useful. Simple brief review points can restate group ownership of the process so far, help the group to put its progress and the process into perspective and reduce unexpected revisiting of issues.

## Selecting tasks, activities, and tools

After outlining the red thread, the facilitator must consider how to move the group through each of these stages. Different activities, different locations, and different work groups can be used to support this progression. In designing each activity within the event, the facilitator must always ensure that it will be appropriate for the "stage" the group will be at, and that it supports the group in moving forward.

At this stage, the "toolkit" of intervention techniques possessed by the individual facilitator becomes important. To select content input to include process and design, the facilitator must:

- Be competent in selecting framing inputs – information and analysis tools – which are potentially relevant and useful to the group in understanding the problem.
- Be competent in matching analysis tools and activities to issues and sources of conflict to ensure that group conflict engagement is productive and not destructive.
- Be capable of selecting specific process inputs appropriate to support group effectiveness.

■ Consciously understand the purpose for which activities are being introduced to the group – is it to promote inquiry or promote advocacy? In other words, is it to question existing beliefs, build new understanding of the issues, or help the group to reach conclusions and decisions?
■ Provide neutrality and objectivity in the selection and analysis of content inputs – ensuring that balanced information and analysis tools are provided to the group which will not unduly favor particular stakeholders.

## Developing a detailed agenda – a practical example

To demonstrate how this works, we explain in detail below the selection of tasks, tools, and activities for a real example of a facilitated process, explaining the purpose and sequencing of each intervention.

The change leader's objective was for the group to develop a new product development process for the organization. After conducting our needs analysis, the outline agenda discussed previously was created and then the following detailed agenda was developed. Appendix 4 contains instructions and detailed explanations of how to use each exercise listed. Here we focus on explaining their selection and purpose in helping the group to work on its task.

Within the detailed agenda example in Figure 2.5 below, we had specific objectives for each individual session:

■ *The change leader briefing:* The CEO of the business unit made a presentation of 30 minutes followed by an open discussion with the group lasting another 30 minutes. The purpose was to ensure that the group had a clear definition of why a new product development process was needed and the strategic context of the task for the business unit – why the business unit's success in solving this problem would be a key driver of the long-term performance of the business.
■ *The facilitator process briefing:* This established the agenda and the logic behind it, and so reassured the group that while it had a challenging task to complete, it had a robust process for working toward a conclusion. Each activity and intervention within the agenda was explained.
■ *Hopes and Fears:* This is an exercise designed to get the group to discuss the undiscussables. By sharing their hopes and fears about the task, group members identified both the critical tasks and the key risks they believed needed to be managed in order to create a new product development process – including hopes and fears about how they would work together as a group.

Importantly, this exercise was selected to send a message to the group that uncertainty is normal. By sharing their fears, group members were also being asked to demonstrate trust in each other, creating a mutual expectation that inquiry and conflict would be conducted constructively.

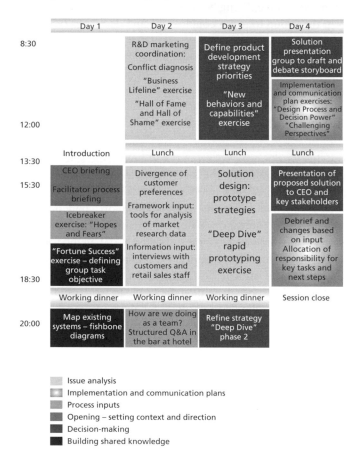

| | Day 1 | Day 2 | Day 3 | Day 4 |
|---|---|---|---|---|
| 8:30 | | R&D marketing coordination: Conflict diagnosis "Business Lifeline" exercise "Hall of Fame and Hall of Shame" exercise | Define product development strategy priorities "New behaviors and capabilities" exercise | Solution presentation group to draft and debate storyboard Implementation and communication plan exercises: "Design Process and Decision Power" "Challenging Perspectives" |
| 12:00 | | | | |
| 13:30 | Introduction | Lunch | Lunch | Lunch |
| 15:30 | CEO briefing Facilitator process briefing Icebreaker exercise: "Hopes and Fears" "Fortune Success" exercise – defining group task objective | Divergence of customer preferences Framework input: tools for analysis of market research data Information input: interviews with customers and retail sales staff | Solution design: prototype strategies "Deep Dive" rapid prototyping exercise | Presentation of proposed solution to CEO and key stakeholders Debrief and changes based on input Allocation of responsibility for key tasks and next steps |
| 18:30 | | | | |
| | Working dinner | Working dinner | Working dinner | Session close |
| 20:00 | Map existing systems – fishbone diagrams | How are we doing as a team? Structured Q&A in the bar at hotel | Refine strategy "Deep Dive" phase 2 | |

Issue analysis
Implementation and communication plans
Process inputs
Opening – setting context and direction
Decision-making
Building shared knowledge

FIGURE 2.5  **Example detailed agenda**

- *Fortune Success:* This is a visioning exercise designed to create a shared ambition for the group and so a shared understanding of its task. It was selected to build some initial cohesion within the group around what it was aiming for and, importantly, what key criteria it would use in decision-making.
- *Mapping existing systems – fishbone diagrams:* This exercise was chosen to help the group share and structure all the knowledge it had about the current product development process within the business, saving time and confusion later by building an adequate and consistent shared understanding of the task and its context.

    Fishbone diagrams are a visually simple way of loosely mapping causal relationships in a business process. Their inexact nature also helps the group and the facilitator – it postpones conflict about the exact causes and interrelationships of issues.

■ *R&D and marketing coordination – conflict diagnosis:* Both the Business Lifeline and Hall of Fame and Hall of Shame exercises were used to focus the group on inquiry – providing tools for reflecting upon, understanding, and analyzing the internal issues causing the need for a new product development strategy:

  – *Business Lifeline* is an exercise to create reflection and learning from past organizational experiences. The purpose is to explore the underlying strengths and weaknesses of the organization.

  – *The Hall of Fame and Hall of Shame* exercise can be used to create reflection and learning from previous experiences of implementing change, and so also explore the underlying strengths and weaknesses of the organization.

  Both these exercises help to create minor conflict in the group, since they force the group to honestly assess the "success" or otherwise of past initiatives (which group members may have initiated, managed or contributed to). The exercises also ensure that this conflict is rarely major, because no choices are required – groups simply need to agree what to add to the list of successes, failures, strengths, and weaknesses of the organization.

  In this facilitation event, the exercises were used to create an inventory of real examples of the problems experienced over the past few years within product development projects. The detailed circumstances of specific examples highlighted points of tension within the existing product development process as outlined in the fishbone diagrams.

■ *Divergence of customer preferences.* Here *framing* was used to explicitly create *inquiry* into the second key cause of the need for a new product development strategy – divergence of customer preferences. Input of information from the market and use of analysis tools facilitated the group in understanding and processing this new information.

  This session's input of new information and opinions created new questions for the group. The explicit purpose was to force group members to review the adequacy of their beliefs (mental models) about the causes of the problems within the current product development process – which were revealed by their fishbone diagrams and interpretation of specific R&D and marketing coordination issues.

■ *How are we doing as a group?* Structured questions guide this discussion, providing the group with a process to make its review of its work more effective and focused. Locating this session in the bar of the hotel provided a change of environment to release tension and give energy to the group.

  Importantly, this session guided group members to review how they were "doing" conflict and what behaviors they needed to change or reinforce in order to continue to engage in productive conflict and avoid descending into destructive conflict when tensions rose.

■ *New Behaviors and Capabilities exercise.* This was used to turn the decisions reached and lessons from the previous exercises into tangible conclusions about priorities, tasks, and required changes. It was used for "framing" what had previously happened in the organization and then translating that understanding into priorities and decision criteria that the group would use in developing and selecting solutions and action plans. The exercise was designed to shift the group to look *forward*.

Conflict here was inevitable and necessary. The exercise required the group to openly make decisions for the first time. It used an analysis tool to help the group to remain in productive conflict, forcing group members to support opinions with logical explanations.

In this case, the exercise was used to help the group to step through a process of defining: which problems within the product development process it considered to be most important; what it believed the key indicators of a competitive new product development process to be and why; what behaviors and capabilities would be required within the organization to overcome those problems and support any better product development process.

In working through this task, the group set some boundaries about what was relevant to spend time discussing and what key features were essential to any solutions and changes to the productive development process.

■ *Solution design – prototyping strategies:* The "Deep Dive" rapid prototyping exercise was used to begin proposing possible solutions and imagining better models for product development for the organization.[11]

In this case, the group tested various ideas about how the product development process could be improved. Importantly, the priorities and decision criteria developed in the morning narrowed the breadth of issues to be considered by the subgroups.

■ *Solution design – selection and refinement of a new product development process:* Part 2 of the Deep Dive exercise forced the group to make some key decisions the previous evening. The shared decision criteria and priorities developed previously enabled it to make faster decisions about which elements of each prototype solution had most potential value.

As always, this task resulted in conflict – if it had not, there would have been cause for concern. The group had to explicitly agree which stakeholder needs it would not satisfy for the "greater good" of the organization. The Deep Dive process helps the group to manage this conflict productively, however all participants have had the opportunity to *voice* their ideas and opinions before decisions are made and the process *integrates* as many good ideas as possible.

■ *Implementation and communication planning:* By this point the group had built a detailed proposal for a new product development process. The task now was to create a foundation for successful implementation of that strategy:

– *Decision Process and Decision Power* is an exercise to help the group do tactical planning about which stakeholders must be consulted to validate, modify, improve, and approve the change agenda. The group used this exercise to develop a plan to win the support of key stakeholders within the business for its new product development process.

– *Challenging Perspectives* is an exercise used to break out of "groupthink" and ensure that the group actively considers the potential beliefs and reactions of other stakeholders. The group used this exercise to review which issues and concerns would need addressing with each stakeholder and how best to answer those questions.

■ *Presentation of proposed solution to the change leader and key stakeholders:* The group presented its recommendations, plus implementation plans and communication plans, to the CEO and key members of the senior management team.

■ *Debrief and allocation of responsibility for next steps:* This is the final, essential task – engaging the group to apply the core disciplines of good implementation: responding to stakeholder input and establishing accountability for key tasks and deadlines.

This process was used to ensure that the group actively responded to feedback received from the senior management team and debated how to adapt their decisions and implementation plans. It was important also to role-model this discipline to the group – to signal that reflecting upon and adapting to ongoing stakeholder inputs is an essential part of effective change implementation.

## Communicating with participants and stakeholders

### Validation of event designs

Review meetings with the change leader and other stakeholders are important throughout the design process. They will help create a mutual understanding and shared ownership of the desired outcomes of the event. They are also useful for solving any problems that may be encountered and determining each party's roles and responsibilities.

There are three basic ways of developing an agenda with a group and stakeholders. The facilitator can:

1. Dictate a facilitator-developed agenda.

2. Facilitate the creation of a group-developed agenda.
3. Present a draft agenda, then review and amend it with the group.

■ *Presenting a draft agenda* and then allowing the group and stakeholders to amend or add to it is highly recommended, as it balances time and expertise in process design with group input to foster ownership of the task and commitment to the process.
■ *Facilitator-developed agendas* provide more control over group effectiveness for the facilitator and are recommended when objectives and tasks are relatively straightforward.
■ *Group-developed agendas* can increase group ownership of the task, but are time-consuming to create and risk setting an inefficient or ineffective agenda, as stakeholders rarely have expertise in facilitation processes.

Groups working without a set of expectations that have been mutually agreed with stakeholders are inherently ineffective. The sooner debates about expectations occur and the greater the depth of real shared understanding and agreement reached between stakeholders, the more quickly the group will be effective in its task.

It is for this reason that effective design and planning of facilitation interventions is so important to creating lasting change. Whenever understanding and management of stakeholder and group expectations can be done before facilitation events, greater group effectiveness and task focus are achieved.

Constant attention to the management of stakeholder expectations before and during facilitation interventions is essential, because the fit between outputs and stakeholder expectations is key to achieving ownership and commitment to change initiatives created.

### Facilitator-developed vs. group-developed agendas
Agendas can be developed either by the facilitator or the group. In most cases, agenda development is a mix of both – the facilitator leading, presenting a draft agenda, and then inviting stakeholders and group members to review it and suggest amendments and additions.

The appropriate balance of facilitator versus group influence on agenda development is different in every case, but understanding the merits of purely facilitator-developed versus group-developed agendas helps to clarify the key issues to consider when deciding how much input to give stakeholders and group members in agenda development.

### Facilitator-developed agendas
Facilitator-developed agendas allow the facilitator to break the overall event objective into sub-parts. This gives participants specific focus for each stage in the event and leads them through a process to address the issues at hand.

Facilitator-developed agendas are also more constraining around the timing and scheduling during the event. The facilitator can plan down to the nth level of detail. This obviously requires more preparation on the behalf of the facilitator; it also requires a greater level of participant trust.

In events where there is a fairly common focus and understanding of issues, where there is little ambiguity, contradiction or conflict in the participant group about the objective and scope of the task, participants can often accept a stricter timescale. In these cases, a facilitator-developed agenda may be appropriate.

### Group-developed agendas

Group-developed agendas can work when it is important for the group to develop a strong sense of ownership of its output – which can in part be fostered by the group controlling its own agenda, rather than having an agenda imposed by an outsider.

Group-developed agendas also work when there are specific issues that need to be dealt with before the group can work cohesively; this may not have been addressed during the event preparation and contracting with participants. Creating a group agenda creates equality – all participants get a chance to air their issues. In addition, if it is unclear at the outset which aspect of the event will be the most important, group-developed agendas can sometimes be more appropriate.

## Managing participant and stakeholder expectations – communication planning

Once the facilitation event is designed, the facilitator and change leader must agree on how they will communicate with participants and other stakeholders before and after the events. If stakeholders are going to be consulted as part of the design phase, this communication planning must begin even earlier.

*Before events*, communication must achieve several things:

■ Clarity about the purpose of the event to all relevant stakeholders.
■ Clarity about what is expected from participants. This ranges from practical details like times and location of attendance to wider issues such as why they have been chosen to attend. It should also provide clarity about the processes and activities to be used during the event in order to reassure participants.
■ Expectations that the event outcomes will be implemented and cause change in the organization – including expected timetables for action.
■ Clarity about future consultation, communication, and involvement of stakeholders in the change initiative.

*After events*, communication must:

- Capture and share the outcomes and conclusions.
- Explain the next steps, including timelines, responsibility for key actions, and who will make final decisions where further or senior approval is required.

**Good communication accelerates groupwork *and* change implementation**

We recently ran two week-long facilitated workshops for the fastest growing business unit of a multinational food company: to develop a new customer retention strategy and renew the innovation process within the business.

Before each workshop, the CEO led meetings with the project teams assigned to each task, and with the senior management team. At each meeting, we explained the agenda and process designed for each group. These meetings provided a forum for an important discussion – the CEO as change leader and the senior management team as key stakeholders voiced their desires, concerns, and rationale for each project.

As well as making the group better informed about its task and therefore accelerating the group process, change leader briefings such as these have an important secondary effect – organizational readiness for change began before the group even embarked upon its task of understanding each problem and designing solutions.

# SECTION 3
# Guiding facilitation events

# Introduction

We have proposed a model of how successful facilitation is dependent upon successful completion of three key steps – event planning, guiding an event and post-event implementation. In this section, we explain the key elements required to *guide* a facilitation event effectively and so to create momentum for change.

As discussed in Section 2, to create real momentum for change, groups must create new solutions based on new insights into the issues and problems. Thus in guiding a facilitation event, the facilitator must help the group to revise its view ("mental model") of the problem, task or situation, to create a new, richer shared mental model, and so envisage and commit to new solutions. As a change leader, once a group enters an event, your ability to influence its success in making these steps is severely limited. The process is in motion, the group has been given autonomy to work within the scope of its task toward its objective and the process is being guided by the facilitator.

However, it is important that you have a strong understanding of what a facilitator should aim to achieve during a facilitation event and how. Understanding the key elements required to *guide* a facilitation event effectively enables you, the change leader:

- To select the right facilitator – you will be better equipped to evaluate a potential facilitator's past experience and their proposed event designs.
- To support the facilitator and the group in their task, providing resources as required but importantly also "ambassadorship" for the group with a wider group of stakeholders. This includes tackling conflict between stakeholder priorities when the group is insufficiently influential to resolve such issues directly.
- If possible, to participate in the facilitation process in a way that promotes group effectiveness.

The role of the facilitator in guiding events is to ensure that groups develop new mental models that both provide valuable new insights and are adequately shared to create coordinated action.[12] This has been described by Hackman[13] and others as "reducing process losses." What he means is establishing and maintaining behaviors which support group effectiveness in working together.

Guiding facilitation events therefore demands competence in:

■ *Establishing objectives and expectations:* Starting facilitation events well by clarifying the task and how the group will work on that task.
■ *Framing:* Using new analysis tools or information to help groups to develop new insights and solutions and to manage conflict.
■ *Conflict engagement:* Helping the group to use productive conflict to engage in inquiry and advocacy.
■ *Closing events well:* Ensuring groups end facilitation events with a clear agenda for action and change.

## Starting facilitation events successfully – clarifying objectives and expectations

The facilitator's primary goal at the start of each event is to define the event correctly – to establish clear objectives for the event and clear expectations of the role of the group. The actions, and ideally the presence, of the change leader are key in achieving this. As a change leader, help with this task is often the first explicit and important support that the facilitator and the group need from you.

Direct briefing of the group task and objectives, the context and scope of that task, and the authority devolved to the group is essential. Wherever possible, you, the change leader, should do this in person, with the whole group and at the start of the group's work.

A useful structure for understanding (and planning) how to start a working event with a group is the "5 Questions" model. The facilitator must ensure that the group gets answers to the following questions:

1. What (will we be working on)?
2. Where (does this fit into the big picture)?
3. Why (are you/we here)?
4. How (will this all work)?
5. When (do we do what, and when do we finish)?

The following sections detail the issues that must be tackled and the questions that must be answered when completing these tasks. Doing this well establishes a foundation for group effectiveness in working together.

Defining the objectives and context – why the task matters – is the first essential activity each group must complete. This ensures that the group has answers to Questions 1, 2 and 3 – what, where and why. Defining how the group will work together is the second essential activity. In doing this, you clarify the expectations of group members as to how they will work together, how the facilitation process will work, and how they will tackle their task. This ensures the group has answers to Questions 4 and 5 – how and when.

## Defining the objectives and context – why the task matters

In order for a group to act effectively in tackling any task, they need to understand the purpose, objectives, and context of that task. In other words, they must have an answer to the questions: "What do we need to achieve? And why?"

"What do we need to achieve?" is often superficially an easy question. But a clear objective requires clarity of expectations about the depth of detail and the breadth of issues which the group must address before the group's objective can be considered to be achieved. For example, "develop a new plan for increasing productivity" might be one team's immediate, shared answer to the question "What do we need to achieve?" But confusion and disagreement quickly arise when the team discusses the level of detail or extent of implementation required of the "new plan."

"Why?" must be answered to give meaning and context to the group's objective. As you will probably have experienced, sometimes the answer to this question is obvious to all, and sometimes it is the source of heated debate. And some groups have no interest or enthusiasm at all for answering it.

For the facilitator intent on fostering real change, discovering or developing a group's answer to this question is essential. Why? Because empowering the group to define the answer creates ownership of the task and is an important first step in the group, building a common shared language and understanding of what the task is.

As a change leader, the briefing you give to the group about its task heavily influences how successful it will be in defining its objectives:

■ If you oversimplify an issue, you signal that the group only requires a superficial understanding of the context of the problem and task. You implicitly encourage it to ignore wider organizational issues when developing recommendations and solutions.
■ But, conversely, you must explicitly define and limit what issues are to be considered. Briefing a group on all the organization's issues simply leaves it feeling impotent and overwhelmed. Groups are easily discouraged by overcomplex tasks. Often it is better for a change leader only to point the group toward an issue, not to explain it. This ensures that the group considers that issue in its work – and with more independence, not yet having heard your interpretation of it.

### Defining the objectives and context – taking time pays off

Our experience is that groups (and facilitators) often underestimate the time required to achieve these two objectives and/or hurry this task – jumping quickly to oversimplified answers with little reflection and debate. The result is false consensus, with differences of opinion within the group about the nature, purpose, and reason for its task remaining unresolved. When this happens, the illusion of progress is short-lived: the questions will inevitably come up for further debate later in the process, and at worst cause the group to revisit many of the decisions and agreements based on its oversimplified understanding of the issues at hand.

"We are here today to increase sales" may be a dramatic and true description of a group's task, but it is also broad and open to misinterpretation – which will obstruct group effectiveness.

"We are here to identify top line growth opportunities, around three key paths: innovation of new products, increasing share of market and increasing size of market in line with the company's growth strategy" might instead create greater clarity of purpose, objectives and context for the group (and other stakeholders).

The group's responses in defining its objectives and context also reveal to the facilitator how much ownership and responsibility members feel for the problem being addressed plus the depth of detail and breadth of issues they consider to be relevant.

### Defining the objectives and context – a process for building group clarity

To define the purpose, objectives, and context of its task and so to begin working effectively, a group must complete two key tasks:

- Understand the needs and expectations of stakeholders.
- Clarify the expectations of the group about outputs and inputs – what they are expected to achieve and what resources they can use in their work.

Importantly, a good needs analysis conducted as part of the event design process described in Section 2 can focus this discussion but cannot replace it. It is always essential to revisit this subject with the group before it begins "work."

### Understanding the expectations of stakeholders

At the start of an event, groups are often very concerned to clarify the expectations of others – particularly what the change leader expects the group to produce. The amount of time a group needs to spend discussing this question during a facilitation event is driven by the complexity of its task and the relative clarity of its briefings by change leaders about the task and about stakeholder expectations.

As discussed in Section 2, good event planning smoothes this process by ensuring that before the event the group receives clear direct answers from both the change leader and other key stakeholders to questions such as "What are we expected to deliver?" and "With what resources, constraints and timescale?"

As a change leader, one of your first opportunities (and responsibilities) to act as an "ambassador" for the group may occur at this time. Your position, status, and network within the organization and outside can often increase the speed, depth, and extent to which the group can get input from stakeholders.

It is not unusual, however, for new issues to be exposed to facilitators only when the group meets. The following example demonstrates this and similar experiences are common to most facilitators, even when good preparatory diagnosis of the organizational and group context has been done.

### Discovering stakeholder expectations within the group sometimes brings unpleasant surprises

Jan, a facilitator in the Netherlands,[14] recently told us about a difficult experience of discovering hidden issues when exploring group objectives and stakeholder expectations at the start of a facilitation event:

We had been asked to facilitate a meeting with a number of project and program managers to increase the consistency and coordination of their communication within their own organizations and with their customers.

At the start of the event, I introduced an exercise I called "bow of tensions," because behind every story line there are tensions, energies or forces that drive the story and the people "in" it.

The group didn't receive the exercise with much enthusiasm. After my short introduction, one of the participants interrupted. He didn't see how our agenda could bring them to a workable solution. Somebody else agreed. Then a discussion arose about our methods and way of working – mind you, we hadn't done a thing yet – and, in the end, about our personalities as facilitators. I was wondering what was going on and why we were getting this extreme reaction.

Everybody expected some or all of the participants to walk out on us. Well, that didn't happen and when it became clear that no one was going to leave, the group finally calmed down.

So I proposed that we should return to the agenda. Again there was some reluctance, but after a long discussion three important and conflicting attitudes emerged within the group. Our task was, of course, to get them all to agree on one course of action, but of the ten people in the group, five believed that they wouldn't be able to find a common course of action; three that the facilitation process was not the way to achieve it; and two that there *was* no common course of action that was relevant to them all.

During this conversation we also discovered that many of the group believed that the projects and programs they were responsible for were impossible: they wouldn't be able to deliver the requested solutions on time *and* they were not able or willing to communicate this to their sponsors. After this exercise we had to make some changes to the agenda and allocate space to explore these issues further.

The "undiscussable" had been made discussable, despite the group's own attempt to prevent this. The program managers had been unable and unwilling to discuss the fact that they already knew their programs would fail, so they had tried a kind of pre-emptive strike: questioning our methods and our capabilities.

By challenging the facilitation agenda, groups can avoid awkward discussions. When this happens, it is the role of the facilitator to take them through this difficult phase.

### Clarifying the expectations of the group about outputs and inputs

Having confirmed its understanding of the expectations of other stakeholders, the group must then build its own shared expectations of what it should aim to achieve, why, how, and with what resources. The group must decide:

- *Outputs* – what it considers to be a feasible objective, how it sees the context of that objective (including which stakeholder needs are most important and why) and what the group thinks "success" for this task will look like.
- *Inputs* – whether the resources available to it are adequate.

The sooner this happens, the more quickly the group will become effective in tackling the task at hand.

### Outputs – objectives and context

Building a shared interpretation of its objectives for the group to start from is a key task of every facilitator. Exercises such as defining a "project Elevator Pitch" (a short statement of the group's objective and the rationale underpinning it) can be useful tools to help a group start (and finish) this conversation.

**Defining objectives and expectations – creating an elevator pitch**

The Elevator Pitch concept comes from the world of venture capital. The idea is that you, an entrepreneur, find yourself in an elevator with a venture capitalist. This is your one chance to sell your business idea to this potential investor and so in only 60 seconds you must define the purpose, key messages and value of your idea, using 100 words or less.

This exercise is often a powerful way of developing a shared understanding within groups of their task and objectives. By defining in a few words the key objective, measures of success, strategic relevance, and most significant challenges in their project, groups create some shared language about their task and some initial agreement about their priorities.

To create a good elevator statement takes time. And people rarely get it right first time. It is useful and necessary for groups to periodically revisit the question of "What are we trying to achieve?" but an exercise such as this provides an important point to refer back to when those discussions are necessary.

An example of an Elevator Pitch exercise is included in Appendix 4.

Often groups also have doubts about the feasibility or the rationale behind a task they have been given. A skilled facilitator will ensure that the group debates those questions enough to be able to start its task with some shared view of its objectives and priorities.

In many situations, facilitated groups are brought together to work on complex problems that a more senior change leader cannot resolve alone. Many groups also instinctively accept an immediate implied responsibility for "solving" problems given to them. Unsurprisingly, therefore, they often feel overwhelmed by their tasks.

This is one of the reasons why devoting time to a change leader briefing of the group task at the start of an event is helpful. The change leader is able to acknowledge as valid the group's questions and doubts and to admit that finding a good solution will be difficult but also to emphasize that *not trying* to find a good solution is unacceptable.

Sometimes groups get "stuck" here and are overwhelmed. We have seen newly formed groups engage in long conversations dedicated to finding the numerous insuperable obstacles to success. While such conversations often help to form group bonds, their contribution to task progress is limited.

Scheduled interim meetings with the change leader help groups and facilitators to avoid this problem. If, by lunchtime on the first day of a week-long facilitation event, the group has convinced itself that it has been given an impossible task, then the thought of coming back to a change leader empty-handed at the end of a week is somewhat daunting and depressing. But if the group has an interim meeting with the change leader on the third day, it has the scope to explore the problem and present a stronger rationale about how and why it should (or should not) commit further work to the project.

### Challenging change leader or stakeholder expectations?

Sometimes a group looks at a task and decides that its priorities, scope and objectives are totally different from those defined by the change leader or other key stakeholders. Often this happens when a group is handed a complex problem. After one or two days spent trying to understand all the issues, a group can become more expert in the problem than the change leader and other stakeholders.

As discussed in Section 2, if it is predictable that this situation might occur, opportunities for ongoing dialogue between the group and the change leader and other stakeholders, for example by telephone or mid-process "update" meetings, should be planned into the facilitation process. Often the facilitator needs to broker these conversations. The purpose of such dialogue is twofold: to enable the group to move forward effectively in its task; and to ensure ongoing stakeholder support of the group's work.

### Objectives and context – a recurring question

Few groups define their objectives only once during a facilitation process. It is useful and necessary to revisit the question of "What are we trying to achieve?" during the event – both to reorientate themselves by reminding themselves of the "big picture" and to help them to build a new mental model of the issue they are working on. As discussed in Section 2, specific time and activities devoted to this work should be built in to the agenda, as should "slack" to allow for impromptu discussions of this question.

As a change leader, you should be prepared for the group to lose momentum periodically and spend time revisiting this question. Make sure you are available to the group both at prearranged times and on an impromptu basis to give them interim *input* (*not* review – you should avoid creating pressure by "judging" incomplete groupwork).

The frequency with which groups revisit the question of their objectives is driven by:

- *The complexity of the group task:* The facilitator cannot control this – but he or she can predict it and use that knowledge when planning the agenda.
- *The depth of real shared understanding and agreement reached by the group regarding its objectives:* Ensuring that the group develops clear shared conclusions from its debates is a key facilitator task within the event. If a group avoids conflict and creates false consensus when

discussing its objectives, it will have to review its objectives again sooner – reducing group effectiveness in the long run.

Groups should (briefly) *document* their objectives, scope and the rationale behind them each time they review their objectives. Often creating a simple bullet point statement on a flip chart will be enough to capture this information. At other times, more detailed notes may be required. What is most important is that the whole group participates in this activity of recording their conclusions. This increases shared clarity, highlights points of difference in group views, and speeds up future debates about objectives and priorities.

### Inputs – adequacy of group resources

Newly formed groups are often keen to question the adequacy of the resources available to complete the task given to them. In most cases, this is a vehicle for group members to express nervousness about the complexity and difficulty of the task. In fact, a group can only assess the adequacy of the resources available when it has defined its objective and, specifically, the scope of its task (the depth of detail and the breadth of issues which it will address).

When the group has defined the scope of its task, then it can and must consider the adequacy of the resources available. Key issues it should take time to clarify are:

■ How much time group members will contribute.
■ How far group members will contribute extra resources to the task (such as using their own budgets or staff time).
■ What extra resources they need from other stakeholders.
■ The feasibility of the group's objective and deadlines given its resources.

When issues become complex or conflict arises, groups which have not explicitly agreed the adequacy of their resources often retreat behind excuses about the feasibility of achieving a result. Excuses about "not knowing enough" are particularly popular – groups insisting they need more information before making a key decision or recommendation.

Planning is one defence against this danger – good needs analysis and event design predict the resources and information that the group will need. Explicit debate and acceptance by the group of the adequacy of the resources and information it possesses at the start of the event is the second key action the facilitator must take to reduce this risk.

## Defining how the group will work together

Defining how the group will work together is the second key task of a facilitator when starting an event. This ensures the group has answers to Questions 4 and 5 of the "5 Questions":

4. How (will this all work)?
5. When (do we do what, and when do we finish)?

In doing this, the facilitator provides clarity for the group by:

- *Defining how they will work together* – ground rules and the group's model of group effectiveness (which we explain below).
- *Clarifying the facilitation process* – how they will work with the facilitator, the change leader, and other stakeholders.
- *Establishing the event agenda* – how they will work on their task.

Defining how a group will work together is an essential element in establishing group effectiveness – the extent to which the group's solution meets or exceeds the standards required within the group and by stakeholders external to the group. In the context of facilitation, group effectiveness is primarily achieved by successfully establishing and maintaining productive group behaviors that enable groups to develop new shared mental models from which new solutions and commitment to change follow.

### Contracting with the group

Ultimately, group facilitation is a powerful means of engaging a group to improve performance, but like any other method it has its limitations. It can only be effective if the group's method of working together is effective. At the start of an event, groups must define their model of group effectiveness – what is required for the group and those supporting them to work together effectively.

Contracting is an agreement between the group and the facilitator about how to work together. It is, most experienced facilitators will tell you, *the* most important process the facilitator can undertake. But to think contracting is done only once is simplistic. The "contract" within a group, including with its facilitator, is constantly tested, renegotiated, and refined as a group works together – both explicitly, with discussion, and tacitly, through behavior.

Initial contracting with a group, when done well, establishes:

- *For group members*, a clear process for how the group is going to work and a clear mechanism to "get back on track" when things do not go according to plan.

■ *For the facilitator*, acceptance by the group of key ground rules which will support group effectiveness and simplify facilitator intervention in the group.

The most explicit element of the contracting process is usually the definition of "ground rules" that the group agrees to observe when working together.

---

### Ground rules – a context-specific model of group effectiveness

Ground rules provide groups with "norms" against which they can judge their behavior and which they can use to call each other to account when someone is behaving outside those norms. Ground rules are an explicit statement of the principles and behaviors the group believes will maintain group effectiveness by helping it to engage in productive conflict and framing.

Every set of ground rules and all "norms" of effective group behavior are *context-specific* – the effectiveness of specific ground rules is always dependent on the situation and the group.

"Being on time" is an example that we constantly encounter of how group ground rules and norms are always context- and organization-specific. Working for the past few years with a global speciality chemical company, we have come to expect that whenever we work with them, everyone always arrives on time, wherever in the world they originate from. Punctuality is not a ground rule that needs to be mentioned, never mind reinforced. Conversely, at a global drinks company we work with, everyone is routinely 10 minutes late – for meetings, for conference calls, for every group session. The "10-minute delay" is so endemic that in their case punctuality is difficult to enforce.

---

For the change leader, there are three ways in which you can exert influence over how the group will work together:

■ *Defining roles within the group:* You may or may not appoint a leader or spokesperson for the group. Equally, you may tell the group members which of them will bear most responsibility for implementing their recommended actions and solutions. In doing so, you create hierarchy and authority within the group. So before doing this, be careful to discuss with the facilitator whether this will help or hinder group effectiveness, given the context of the task and the group.

   If, as change leader, you are also a group member, think hard too about what role you should play within the group and how you will signal this. For example, recently we facilitated an advisory group deciding the R&D

strategy of a small telecommunications technology company. The chairman of the board was a member of the group, but did not consider himself an expert in the subject. To signal this and take low authority within the group, he actively sought briefings and additional explanations of issues from other group members before, during and after each session.

■ *Defining your own role as change leader:* How you behave with the group and what behaviors you expect of them will affect group effectiveness. For example, in some organizations, expecting a very formal, structured communication process between you and the group is helpful. Transparency and formality of process can create efficiency. Equally, however, for other tasks and organizations, such formality is inefficient, creating a burden of rework and documentation that adds little value.

■ *Defining the responsibilities and relationships of group members to other stakeholders:* For example, is a group member responsible for representing their boss and departmental colleagues? Will you "protect" them if they propose a solution that will cause painful change in their own team? (and if so, how?)

### "Generic" ground rules – some underlying principles

Many writers on facilitation propose specific ground rules as essential to group effectiveness. We find both valuable insights and debatable points in every set of generic ground rules. We particularly like Schwarz's rules – because they are grounded in principles to promote productive behaviors that reinforce group effectiveness.[15] Schwarz's rules, which we extend with the last point, and their impact on the facilitation process are summarized in Table 3.1 below.

### Process for contracting

The process of explicitly contracting with groups to establish ground rules is essential because:

■ Facilitators can intervene in the group process and structure to improve performance only if they have authority within the group and willingness on the part of participants to change.
■ Authority within the group is required as changes may affect the broader organizational context and other stakeholders may not agree to the changes proposed.
■ If the group is unwilling to engage in change due to a lack of perceived choice, comfort level or other factors, facilitation may not work.

Understanding and affirming the ground rules also empower groups and individuals, since once they understand what is expected of them, participants can then act within these boundaries.

TABLE 3.1 Ground rules to promote group effectiveness

| Ground rule | Impact on facilitation process and group effectiveness |
| --- | --- |
| 1. Test assumptions and inferences<br><br>2. Share all relevant information<br><br>3. Explain your reasoning and intent | Engage in and enable *inquiry* – both in the designing, guiding and participating in facilitation events. In doing so, fully understand relevant information, ideas, analysis and conclusions and so make *conflict* more informed and more productive. |
| 4. Use specific examples and agree on what important words mean | To be effective, facilitators, change leaders, and participants require *clarity*. For example, if the group defines "revenue growth" as a key performance measure, it must define what revenue growth means and how it should be calculated. Is revenue growth measured in local currency or US dollars? How will exchange rate fluctuations be treated? |
| 5. Focus on interests, not positions | Interests express the needs or desires of particular stakeholders – exploring them is a process of *inquiry*. Positions are views on how needs or interests should be met, that is, *advocacy* of particular solutions. Focusing too much on positions moves a group toward premature advocacy and so destructive conflict. |
| 6. Combine advocacy and inquiry | To reach shared decisions and new mental models, group participants have a responsibility to both engage in debate and draw conclusions within the group. |
| 7. Jointly design next steps and ways to test disagreements | Participants have a responsibility to *engage* with each other and key stakeholders to ensure that action plans are based on an adequately shared new mental model. |
| 8. Discuss undiscussable issues | Accept *conflict as positive* and beneficial for the organization, not as something to be avoided. |
| 9. Use a decision-making rule that generates the level of commitment needed | Do not "limit" the *organizational context* artificially, as this will reduce the real value and relevance of solutions and decisions.<br><br>Consider implementation requirements as well as quality of solution when decision-making. Feasibility and enrolment are key to successful implementation. |
| 10. Ensure both the practical and political feasibility of solutions | The group must not lose sight of the organizational context and has a responsibility to live within that reality. |

SOURCE: Adapted from Schwarz (2002)

How long you spend "contracting" is directly related to the length of time that the group is going to be working together. If you are facilitating a short two- or three-hour event, an hour on contracting is counterproductive. However, if you are going to be facilitating an event that lasts for a number of days or which consists of a group that will meet regularly over a longer time span, then it can be worth spending longer on this process.

### When setting ground rules, balance facilitator expertise and group ownership

Debate exists as to whether ground rules are best developed by groups or imposed upon them. Underneath this debate is essentially a question as to what has the greater influence on group effectiveness – "ownership" of the ground rules or their "quality." A facilitator's answer to this question will define whether they choose to start events by defining for the group how it will work together or by facilitating a debate within the group about how it wants to work together.

1. *Presenting draft ground rules* and then allowing the group to amend or add to them is highly recommended. One technique we often find effective is to use the distinction of different types of ground rules to both impose rules and give the group ownership of them:

   ■ Ground rules about values – such as the duty to honestly share opinions, the duty to respect others' views, and so on – can be imposed as the minimum standards expected of groups in order for the facilitator to be effective. The facilitator can then invite the group to add to these values.

   ■ Procedural ground rules – when the group will meet, what roles people will play, and so on – can be defined by the group.[16] The facilitator need only be concerned with these rules if they conflict with his or her model of group effectiveness.

2. *Developing ground rules with the group from scratch*, we do not recommend – because this reduces the probability of the group defining ground rules which support group effectiveness.

3. *Dictating ground rules* disempowers groups and so is only recommended when there is a very large group or severe time restrictions, or if strong conflict between different members of the group is anticipated, in which case the facilitator may wish to dictate the ground rules to prevent the group getting "stuck" on the contracting process.

### Clarifying group expectations of the facilitator

To work together effectively, groups must also understand the facilitator's role and relationship to the group – what the group can expect the facilitator to contribute to its work and the facilitation process.

Importantly, in establishing group expectations of their role, facilitators should:

- Establish their role and contribution within the group as a process expert – helping the group to work together more effectively.
- Clarify group expectations about facilitator neutrality – a facilitator must be neutral about *what* the group decides but has a duty to influence *how* it works together.

Taking the time to be transparent with the group about how the facilitation process "works" has multiple benefits, both for the facilitator and for groups. Transparency enriches the group members' ability to:

- Understand the facilitation process and so the underlying purposes of the agenda and ground rules for group effectiveness – and so to consciously choose to behave in ways that support them.
- Problem-solve and operate within groups more effectively in the future, with or without facilitator support, by applying the underlying principles of effective facilitation.

As Schwarz highlights,[17] such "developmental facilitation" requires more time and facilitator skill but is more likely to result in fundamental change – because groups have more ownership of the process and can act with greater autonomy.

For example, once a group understands the difference between inquiry and advocacy – and the benefits of separating these processes when analyzing information – group members can and often will intervene to stop each other from deciding too quickly about how to act on new information.

### Establishing the agenda – how the group will work on their task

After outlining the event – putting the group task and objectives in context, and helping the group to define how they will work together, the next key task in starting an event well is establishing an agenda which supports the group's work.

Agendas provide a road map for events and let the group think about the upcoming tasks, increasing their confidence about their ability to complete their assignment.

In many cases, it is better if the agenda presented to the group is not too detailed. Too much specificity can lead the group to expect that the work of completing the task at hand will be relatively straightforward and painless and/or reduce the facilitator's flexibility to adapt the agenda in response to the group's progress.

Group "review" of the agenda can and should happen at multiple points throughout the facilitation event – some planned and some unplanned. Equally, review should occur both at a macro- and a micro-level – how the group will spend the next day and how the group will spend the next hour.

## During events – essential elements for creating real momentum for change

Designing, planning, and starting events well are all important foundations which create the potential for change to occur. But it is *during* events that the depth and impact of facilitation is created, that, with the help of the facilitator, the potential for change is translated into momentum for change.

In the sections that follow we discuss in more detail what a facilitator must do in order to:

■ Challenge existing mental models.
■ Facilitate conflict engagement.

Particular attention is given in this section to handling key difficult moments when groups risk losing commitment or descending into negative behaviors and destructive conflict.

For the change leader, this deeper understanding of the processes of framing and conflict engagement will give you greater insight into how the facilitator is working with a group and so an ability to make a more informed assessment of the quality of the facilitator's work.

### Framing: Challenging mental models

The central task of any facilitated event within a change initiative is to create an improved and shared solution to an existing problem. Groups and individuals come to a facilitation event with an existing "mental model" – an understanding of the problem. That mental model is built on their personal experience of the problem and/or their understanding of the scope and task as defined for them by other stakeholders. For a facilitation event to contribute to solving the problem, it must help the group to create an *improved* solution. For this to happen, framing must occur – some form of redefinition or re-evaluation of the problem and how the group individually and collectively understands it. To come to a new understanding of the problem they face, a group must either accept and interpret new information or revise their interpretation of previously held information by analyzing it in new ways. Thus to support change a facilitator must intervene to challenge the existing mental models through which the group views the problem, task or situation. To achieve this, a facilitator must understand how introducing new information or new analysis tools can help the group to understand or solve the problem it is tackling. In addition, a facilitator must understand when he or she can, must and must not intervene in framing in order both to contribute to group effectiveness and to remain substantively neutral regarding group outcomes. Facilitators are neutral about the decisions groups make but not neutral about the *processes* groups use to reach those outcomes and decisions.

During the process of framing, the change leader has a responsibility to *postpone judgment* and *remain open-minded*. Why?

■ Because at the start of their work, the change leader often knows more than the group about the problem. As such, the change leader often has an existing conscious or unconscious prejudice toward accepting a particular solution. ("It keeps breaking and is expensive to fix. We should buy a new one.")

■ But by the end of their work, a group often knows more about the problem or issue than the change leader – and the change leader must accept this if a better solution is to be found. ("Yes, it's broken, but that's because there's a design fault. A new one will break as often. We should repair and upgrade it instead.")

The following sections explore the process and management of framing in more detail.

### Two ways to challenge existing mental models

Groups and individuals come to a facilitation event with an existing mental model precisely because they have some information about the problem and have used some mental models for analyzing that information.

There are two tools that change leaders will see facilitators use with groups to prompt them to re-evaluate their existing mental models or framing of a situation – input of new information and input of new analysis tools:

■ "Information" is data which may be relevant to understanding or solving the problem the group is tackling. It includes facts, opinions, and interpretations.

■ "Analysis tools" are techniques for analyzing information – both new information and existing information.

Information inputs promote inquiry. They:

■ Ensure groups have an adequate base knowledge about their task.
■ Challenge the group to question the adequacy of their existing mental models.

Analysis tools can promote either inquiry or advocacy. Depending on the particular tool, they:

■ Assist the group in testing the adequacy of their existing understanding of the problem (inquiry).
■ Help the group to develop new or revised understandings of the problem (advocacy).
■ Help groups to manage their decision-making processes – making the process of advocacy within the group more transparent and so more robust.

As a change leader, you will see facilitators introduce new information and analysis tools to the group from four basic sources:

■ External third parties.
■ Third parties internal to the organization.
■ Group members.
■ The facilitator.

### Managing the process of framing
To help the group build new shared mental models, the facilitator must manage the process of framing – how the group challenges its existing mental models and considers new ones – so that this occurs in a way that supports group effectiveness.

### Introducing new information and analysis tools
As discussed in Section 2, when engaging with a change leader, group and organization, a facilitator has a responsibility to assess their competence to work with the particular issue at hand – based on the complexity and nature of the problem. A change leader must understand that a facilitator is not and cannot be entirely neutral because, in designing and guiding events, he or she will influence *what* information and analysis tools input is (and is not) given to groups in events and *by whom*. However, he or she can and must support an effective group process and group autonomy by ensuring that the group is provided with balanced information and analysis tools which will not unduly favor particular stakeholders' views.

Input is perceived as more or less neutral depending on its source because groups accord different levels of neutrality and objectivity to different stakeholders. Group members' input tends to be perceived as less neutral than the input of a third party. Analysis tools are perceived as more neutral than information because they place emphasis on how the group should evaluate information, but not what information the group should value. Figure 3.1 summarizes the relative neutrality of different inputs.

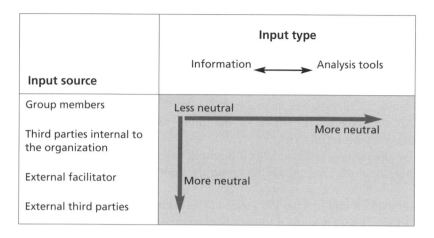

FIGURE 3.1 The relative neutrality of different types and sources of inputs to groups

Whilst facilitators must have some competence to select relevant information and analysis tool inputs, their role and authority in relation to group process will be damaged if the group perceives them as (or perceives them to view themselves as) "content" experts.

Thus, in managing the introduction of input to the group, a facilitator should, whenever possible:

- Facilitate inputs by third parties – using new information and analysis tools attributable to independent parties.
- Provide analysis tools rather than information, because these have higher perceived neutrality.

As a change leader, it is useful to understand that while input by third parties can be helpful, you are often not the best source of such inputs. Certainly a change leader briefing at the start of the project can and should provide lots of information to the group. But the group must receive as many inputs as possible from other sources, both in order to perceive that independent, new solutions are required and to increase their ability to develop insights on the problem that are new to you, the change leader.

*Managing input of information and analysis tools by facilitators*
When information or an analysis tool is introduced directly by the facilitator, he or she should:

- Always confirm permission from the group to introduce them: "May I share something with you that may be useful in helping you to think about this."
- Remain emotionally detached from the information and analysis tools that are being introduced. If a group places little value on information or a tool a facilitator gives them, he or she should not take it personally.
- Explain to the group why he or she thinks the information or analysis tools may be useful to it.
- Use storytelling and examples if possible when sharing information and analysis tools. These show the group the context within which it might use new information or tools.
- Get explicit buy-in from the group of the usefulness of particular analysis tools before pushing it to spend substantial time using them.

**Choices give autonomy to groups**
One technique we often use to ensure that groups maintain some sense of autonomy and so ownership of their conclusions is to give them choices over the analysis tools they use.

Sometimes, we give them explicit choices. For example, working with a group to analyze their product's competitive advantages in the semiconductor market, we explained two techniques. One was mapping the "value curve" (value chain and business models) of their main competitors. The other compared their product performance against a number of key attributes valued by customers and against the priority attached to each attribute by each customer segment. The group then discussed the relative advantages of each tool and decided to use the second technique, seeing it as more useful to them.

Sometimes we let groups make implicit choices. "Stacked" tasks are one way of doing this – giving groups a large block of time to complete several tasks. For example, we worked with a small group from a construction company to develop a strategy for growing its toll-road business. We dedicated a whole afternoon to comparing alternative joint venture partnership models, evaluating potential partners, and selecting a preferred partnership model and target potential partners.

At the start of the afternoon, we presented and explained a tool for each

task. But we gave no guidelines about how much time to spend on what –
this was left to the group to decide, with the result that they also decided the
relative importance of each task.

**Serving the tea – subtle ways to de-emphasize facilitator input**
Recently we had the opportunity to observe an excellent experienced facilitator of outdoor team-building exercises at work.

Throughout the day Victoria, the facilitator, guided her group through a
series of complex challenges – each requiring the group to both determine
and implement a solution to a problem.

After each challenge the group retreated indoors to debrief its performance.
When debriefing, they sat in a circle, drinking tea and eating biscuits. And
one specific, subtle thing that Victoria did when guiding the debrief caught
our eye. Whenever she challenged the group with a question, she remained
in her chair or stood up. But whenever she voiced her opinion or interpretation, she knelt – moving forward to offer more tea to members of the
group, particularly those most challenged by what she was saying.

*Managing input of information or analysis tools by group members*
Group members often do not all possess the same information about the
group's task, because of their different expertise, experience or access to
information within or outside the organization. For example, sales and
marketing staff often have more knowledge than finance staff of why
specific products are best sellers, but finance staff may know more about
why those products are more or less profitable than others. As such, an
important element of managing framing is often managing the process of
how and when group members share with each other what they know about
the problem at hand. In managing this form of input, facilitators should
wherever possible:

■ Identify in advance the contributions (knowledge and skills) that each
  group member may bring to the group. (This has been discussed in more
  detail with group selection and diagnosis in Section 2.)
■ Plan when and how contributions will be shared within the group. As a
  basic principle "sooner is better."

The facilitator should also explicitly separate contributions of information by group members from their statements of opinion. For example, he or she should:

- When a specific activity is being used to share group members' knowledge about the problem, remind participants to distinguish for their colleagues what they *know* and what they *think*.
- Summarize group members' contributions. Use this as an opportunity to reinforce distinctions between what they *know* and what they *think:* "So Jan is saying the *Boston matrix is a tool to categorize products* within a product life cycle and you *think it could be useful* in setting priorities for R&D investment."
- Actively remind group members to *withhold judgment* when appropriate – waiting for more information or analysis before forming opinions. This must be done during the event, but is also supported by the group's ground rules. Explaining to groups how learning occurs – that gathering new information, creating new shared mental models, and then taking decisions and action are sequential, separate steps in problem-solving – can also help groups to learn to defer judgment of each other's contributions.

For a facilitator, membership of the group is based on process expertise – as such, facilitators have a duty to influence the *process* of *how* information is input and analyzed in the group events. To ensure groups *use* information and analysis tools *effectively*, they must ensure that the group:

- Understands the information and analysis tools available to it.
- Agrees which analysis tools it will use.
- Uses the analysis tools correctly to analyze the information available.

Thus for the change leader observing the work of facilitators, it is important to be aware that having helped the group to complete these tasks, the facilitator also has a duty *not to influence what the group concludes* as a result of the process of accepting and analyzing new information. Their only responsibilities when the group is using tools to analyze information are to ensure the group:

- Has productive conflict and debate in analyzing the information available before reaching conclusions.
- Reaches clear conclusions and decisions based on its analysis of the information available.

Both steps are achieved by ensuring that the group observes effective processes in how they conduct conflict and make decisions.

## Facilitating conflict engagement

### *Conflict must occur for mental models to change*

As we have seen, to come to a new understanding of the problem and create a new shared mental model, the group must challenge its existing mental models, create new ones, and make decisions.

When individuals and a group create new shared mental models, they change or reject ideas that they previously believed were "true" and accept new ideas about how issues seen as relevant to the problem are related. In doing so, they change how they evaluate issues, how they think and feel about them – inquiry and then advocacy occur. Making these changes is difficult and necessarily involves conflict, as it requires old values and beliefs to be challenged and found inadequate.

Conflict engagement is essential for this process of inquiry and advocacy to occur. This means exploring differences in group values, views, and behaviors in order to help the group to develop new shared mental models.

As such, conflict is an essential element of every facilitated event. The only question for the facilitator to manage is: How does that conflict occur? Is it denied, avoided and postponed, or acknowledged and tackled? Is it explicit or disguised? Is it emotionally charged or a rational intellectual debate (at least, on the surface)?

*How* the group engages with this conflict is crucial, since productive conflict allows group members to explore different interpretations of issues, values, and behaviors without substantial process losses.

Conflict can, however, increase or destroy group effectiveness:

- *Productive conflict* provides a robust challenge to the group's diverse interpretations of the information and issues before building commonly understood conclusions and decisions about how to move forward.
- *Destructive conflict* disables a group, destroying its sense of shared purpose and ownership of its task.

---

### Conflict – a definition

Despite a lack of consensus among academics, there are some common themes among the definitions of conflict:[18]

- Conflict is based in perceived differences. Of course the perceived difference may not be real, but conversely if the difference is real but not perceived, there is no conflict.

- There is interdependence among parties (that is, each has the potential to interfere with the other).

■ There are issues of blockage, opposition, and scarcity. When one party
blocks the means to a goal or interest of another, a state of conflict exists.

In this section we explore how to facilitate productive conflict. Facilitators help the group by doing three key things:

■ Clarifying the sources of conflict – discovering the differences between group members' views, values or behaviors that are creating conflict.
■ Providing processes and interventions for exploring conflict and channeling it into solutions – to help the group move through conflict more effectively. As such, framing is an effective tool for helping groups to engage in productive conflict and avoid descending into destructive conflict.
■ Helping the group to engage in productive conflict and avoid destructive conflict – by influencing the behavior of group members during conflict.

The responsibility – and possibly the most challenging role – of the facilitator is to enable the group to engage in productive conflict and prevent it from descending into destructive conflict.

The kinds of behaviors exhibited in productive and destructive conflict are, when extreme, significantly different. Table 3.2 provides some examples of the differences.

TABLE 3.2 Productive and destructive conflict

| Productive conflict | Destructive conflict |
|---|---|
| Acknowledges and values conflict as a necessary part of the progress of groups in developing solutions to problems | Sees conflict as a negative process – as something to be avoided and as a signal that a group is failing to make progress |
| Is explicit in both the causes and goals of conflict | Disguises participants' causes of disagreement or ambitions |
| Is anchored by a focus on specific issues | Tackles broad, general issues or "jumps" from one topic to another |
| Uses facts and explicit reasoning to support opinions | Values strength of emotion above reasoning and evidence |

### Clarifying the sources of conflict

To engage in productive conflict, a group first needs to know what it is (really) arguing about. To achieve this, the facilitator must help the group *explore* and *identify* the sources of its conflict.

Conflict can come from an enormous variety of apparent sources: ambiguity around expectations, changes in leadership or direction or roles, participants trying to manage problems outside their control, or external parties applying restrictions to their ability to solve problems.

In fact, there are three root causes of conflict:

1. *Scarce resources:* Conflict between parties over who will possess, control or use resources.
2. *Collective procedures and/or policies:* Conflict over the coordination of results, or control of group activities.
3. *Role behaviors of individuals:* Expectations of what individual members should and should not do.

As many facilitators and change leaders know, however, discovering the root causes of conflict can be difficult. Often conflict over one issue is used as a vehicle to express hidden conflicts about other issues – some of which may even be unconscious in the minds of the protagonists. Finding the real root causes of conflicts can be emotionally hard work for all parties, takes time, and often has many moments of false hope – followed by more conflict and inquiry.

Where conflicts are more complex, it is usually for one of three reasons:

- The reasoning behind one or more parties' positions is complex and difficult for other parties to comprehend.
- One or more parties cannot fully articulate the rationale guiding their (strongly held) position – "gut feeling" is a classic example of this.
- One or more parties are unwilling to state the real reasoning behind their position – often because of organizational politics.

When this is the case, exploring conflict requires both more time and more sophisticated facilitator interventions. This is why framing is such an important facilitation tool.

### Uncovering root causes of conflict – a recent example

Last year we were working with a growing division of a leading fast-moving consumer goods company, helping a group of senior managers from across the business to develop a new customer engagement and retention strategy. The senior managers were colleagues, but not a team – they represented diverse functions within the business and few had any overlapping responsibilities.

Initially, we encountered problems with engagement in the process. Several senior sales managers repeatedly questioned the value of the project and the facilitation process. In their minds, they had an answer already and knew how the market should be tackled. The root cause of conflict seemed to be item 2 above – conflict over control of group activities.

Later, however, having "signed up" to the process, conflict arose because some of the same senior salespeople were behaving disruptively. Conflict seemed to have moved onto item 3 – role behaviors of individuals.

Having resolved these issues, however, conflict continued at an unusually intense level – focused on customer segmentation and how the market should most appropriately be analyzed. The conflict seemed again to be item 2 – control of group activities.

At the end of the week, when the group presented its findings to the top management team, the management had the same discussion about how best to analyze the market and segment their customer base and fought in front of the group. This was a sign that the issue had remained unresolved for a long time … and the "winners" would control the executive team. The conflict had infected *all* relationships between the sales and marketing functions throughout the organization. The real conflict was item 1 – control of scarce resources. Members of the group were expressing opinions and "fighting" on behalf of their bosses – and they were themselves largely unconscious of this.

### Assessing the cost–benefit of conflict (and conflict avoidance)

Not all group conflict is productive. Some conflict issues are simply not important enough relative to the group's task to justify spending group time in exploring and resolving them. Equally, some conflicts are so deep and complex that if the group tackles them, it may never move forward and/or it may do unjustifiable damage to the organization or particular stakeholders.

Facilitators, despite usually having a more positive appetite for conflict engagement than most individuals, have a responsibility to identify when the cost–benefit of exploring particular conflicts is not justified. When this happens, however, it is important that the facilitator explicitly agrees with the group, and in some cases with the change leader, that the particular conflict will not be tackled.

### Balancing cost–benefit – sometimes a decision for the team, the change leader and not the facilitator

Recently we worked with the European leadership team of a successful pharmaceutical company. They came to us for a week-long program with an explicit agenda to address how functions in the European head office should be realigned following a Europe-wide build-up of matrix organizations to replace the previous system of national affiliates (a major change process).

Informal briefings before the program, however, revealed that underneath the question of alignment, there was a bigger question: Why were communication and coordination within the team poor? What were the barriers to greater team effectiveness?

Over the course of the week, these hidden issues became more apparent as the team explored what was needed for it to best support the new matrix organization beneath it. But in the words of one of our colleagues: "They walked up to the swimming pool, stood at the edge for a long time, looked hard at the deep water, and then decided to walk away." The deeper, more difficult issues were avoided.

Practical steps, action plans, and priorities for change in their formal structures were agreed. But the group chose not to explore some problems about how they worked as individuals and as a team. Whenever these issues arose, individuals quickly changed the subject of the discussion.

Several months later, a follow-up meeting revealed that, since our program, the team was in fact working together much better and communicating more effectively. Despite avoiding confronting some of the root causes of its conflict, the group had implemented the formal changes and action plans with positive effects.

Privately, we expressed some surprise. But this experience provided an important reminder for us that ultimately the decision to engage in conflict must come from the group and the change leader. It is the group, not the facilitator, who must live with the long-term consequences of exploring deep conflicts in the group or organization.

### Diagnosing productive vs. destructive conflict

Once a group has begun to debate an issue, it is always important for the facilitator to assess whether it is engaged in productive or destructive conflict.

For you as change leader, this ability to distinguish productive and destructive conflict engagement is also important – particularly when you are a member of the group or have the opportunity to observe the group at work.

Destructive conflict reduces the quality of the solution produced and then raises the question for the change leader of whether destructive conflict within the group was inevitable or whether a more skilled facilitator might have been able to guide the group into more productive conflict engagement.

To diagnose productive versus destructive conflict engagement, it can be useful to consider what specific group behaviors are being observed:

- How are individuals contributing? Are they exchanging points of view?
- How is the group interacting? How is it developing? Is it creating shared mental models?
- How is the group making decisions? What is the quality of those decisions?
- How are organizational decisions made? Are group processes and behavior aligned or in conflict with wider organizational processes? Is the group adequately challenging the status quo? Is the group sufficiently aligned with key stakeholders to get something done?

Answering these questions then provides a basis for answering the core question a facilitator must face when groups are in conflict: How destructive or productive is this conflict? No group conflict is ever totally productive, nor entirely destructive. The reality is a spectrum. Therefore in the face of any conflict, the facilitator must consider: How big are the process losses for the group? And how important are those process losses? If the group is in destructive conflict over where to eat dinner, the process losses tend not to matter and can even be productive – letting off steam and tension. If the conflict is about implementation priorities, then small process losses can matter. Destructive conflict is therefore context-specific.

### When destructive conflict occurs, group effectiveness declines and "process losses" increase

The key indicators of destructive conflict are substantial "process losses" – evidenced by low application of skill and knowledge to the task, a decline in the group's performance and capability, and group members experiencing a high level of frustration from participation.

Process losses are also always context-related – what level of group effectiveness and what level of process losses are inevitable and "normal" are influenced by the group structure and organizational context. "Effective group processes" must be defined in the context of the group, the individuals within it, and the wider organizational context. Group effectiveness is, as explained earlier, the extent to which the group's solution meets or exceeds the standards required from within the group and by stakeholders external to the group.

**Conflict engagement is required to create real group effectiveness**

In most cases, destructive outcomes of conflict are recognized more than conflict's potential benefits. These outcomes include hostility within the group, misperception, hardened antagonistic positions, and emotional exhaustion, and frequently lead to low productivity, less efficiency, less effectiveness, and failure to achieve organizational objectives.

Withdrawal might not be encouraged, but often both groups and facilitators seeking consensus encourage smoothing (emphasizing areas of agreement and de-emphasizing areas of difference) and compromising (searching for solutions that bring some degree of satisfaction to the conflicting parties).

Such behavior does not, however, resolve conflicts. To achieve group effectiveness requires conflict engagement:

> Conflict engagement, as opposed to mere management or settlement, points to an outcome that, in the view of the parties involved, is a permanent solution to the problem. [19]

One of the key developmental challenges for many facilitators is first to accept this concept themselves and then to succeed in persuading groups to accept it and its impact on what constitutes a positive outcome from conflict.

---

**Change leaders impact conflict engagement**

As a change leader, you should be aware that your actions can often strongly help or obstruct a group from engaging in productive conflict.

Questions of scope are a classic source of change leader influence over group conflict. For example, to save time, you may tell a group that it is not necessary to consider certain topics or stakeholder needs.

Recently, developing a strategy for a new business unit of a technology start-up, we were asked only to ensure good alignment with one of the two existing business units. The view of the board was that there was little benefit in ensuring strong alignment with the second existing business unit. And the working group assigned to the project agreed. In that case, the change leaders (the board) effectively suppressed potential conflict over an issue with low cost–benefit.

Several years ago, however, we worked with a group planning the consolidation of its payments processes into a shared service center for a large shipping and transportation group. Consideration of the impact on sales and invoicing processes was defined as out of scope. But stakeholders in key

business units could not accept that payment processes could be consolid-
ated independently of invoicing processes. It became apparent that the
cost–benefit of this conflict avoidance (around consolidating invoicing
processes) was too high. The change leader – the group CFO – had to be
persuaded to broaden the scope of the project (and to extend his timeline
and budget for it).

## Helping the group to engage in productive conflict

The extent to which a group achieves positive versus negative benefits from
conflict is driven in large part by its behaviors in response to conflict.
Whether it succeeds in moving from conflict to reaching agreement is
closely related to how individuals view the conflict process and how groups
handle the conflict itself.

Here, the role of the facilitator is to work with the group to maximize the
positive benefits of conflict while minimizing the negative outcomes upon
the group and organization. Thus where the facilitator has diagnosed the
causes of a conflict, assessed the cost–benefit of exploring that conflict, and
identified a useful tool to help the group work through it, he or she must then
manage the group's behavior during conflict.

The facilitator can provide processes and interventions to explore
conflict. There are two key ways for him or her to help the group to engage
in productive conflict:

- *Moving from inquiry to advocacy* helps groups to explore the causes of
  conflict and channels them into decisions.
- *Maintaining ground rules* helps depersonalize conflict.

### Moving from inquiry to advocacy

Analysis tools provide systematic methods for analyzing issues, and so help
groups by providing processes for:

- Engaging in inquiry – enriching their understanding of each other's
  mental models.
- Engaging in advocacy – creating new, shared mental models and making
  decisions based on this shared understanding.

A number of exercises for each of these processes are given below, and
details can be found in Appendix 4.[20]

TABLE 3.3 **Some sample exercises**

| Inquiry – example exercises exploring causes of conflict | Advocacy – example exercises channeling conflict to decisions |
|---|---|
| Hopes and Fears | Fortune Success |
| Business Lifeline | Elevator Pitch |
| Hall of Fame and Hall of Shame | New Behaviors and Capabilities |
| Challenging Perspectives | Decision Process and Decision Power |
| How Are We Doing as a Team? | Beat Yourself: Option 2 – responding to competitive attacks |
| Beat Yourself: Option 1 – understanding competitors | |

At times, groups engage in advocacy too quickly and thereby reach a "false" agreement which may hide differences in mental models. Facilitators will often have to judge whether individuals are not really sharing their beliefs. Then it becomes necessary to take a step back from advocacy and move back into inquiry.

---

**When the group jumps to a solution or conclusion too fast**

This often happens when the group has a need to feel it is making progress, is too reliant on one or two participants, or simply wants to avoid conflict, choosing instead withdrawal (one party retreating from conflict), smoothing (de-emphasizing areas of disagreement) or compromising (prioritizing mutual acceptability in selecting solutions).

In these circumstances the facilitator needs to introduce some structured process to evaluate and critique the solution or conclusion. Making the group answer the following questions often provides an entry point to do this:

■ What will the stakeholders say?

■ Who will resist this solution? Why? What can we do to reduce resistance?

■ What will this solution cost in terms of time and money? Is it the most cost-effective solution?

---

### Maintaining ground rules

When groups are struggling with complex conflicts, the facilitator needs to support the group in observing its own ground rules so that it is able to handle the emotional tension of conflict for longer and depersonalize conflict as far as possible. When this occurs, the group then has more time and ability to explore the sources of its conflict. In other words, more inquiry can occur.

Reinforcement of ground rules is a classic and reliable technique for facilitators to challenge observed unproductive behaviors by the group in response to conflict.

Independent of the process used by the facilitator, participants must feel that they have all been treated equally and ethically. To achieve this, the conflict engagement process must have observed the ground rules agreed within the group and used decision-making processes acceptable to at least the majority of the group.

Perceived equity is lost during the facilitation process if participants win or lose an "unfair" fight. Group disengagement from the process and the task soon follows. This frequently happens if equity in decision-making is promised but then withdrawn when key decisions need to be made.

Most groups are experienced in working in situations of unequal status and authority in their daily work and can accept a situation where some members have greater influence on decisions – provided that this is established upfront as an expectation of how the group will work together.

---

**When the group refuses to have an opinion or cannot agree – strategies to help the group make choices with perceived equity**
Open discussion and dialog can help a group to work through issues, but in many cases, the emotions and feelings of members can get in the way of moving the decision-making process forward. And issues of power, status, and authority can result in an unbalanced analysis of issues.

Using strategies that help a group visually make choices can be helpful. Here are some ideas to consider that force the group to make choices:

- *Coloured stickers:* Group members are given sticky note pads with a colour coding scheme, for example red means first choice, yellow second and green third. Each group member prioritizes the issues, ideas or action and sticks a note beside it. The facilitator calculates the points and identifies priorities.

- *Straw voting:* Each participant is given a number of straws to vote with. The number of straws is less than the number of issues. Participants walk around the room and place a straw on issues of importance. The facilitator then counts the straws.

> ■ *Take it off the table:* Perhaps there are too many issues being discussed or the group feels overwhelmed. At this point, take some of the issues "off the table." Again this can be done by simple voting or using one of the above methods.

## Intervening to defuse destructive conflict

A facilitator can and must help the group to establish and maintain behaviors and relationships which support the group effectiveness when under stress, that is, to avoid or escape destructive conflict.

To do this, facilitators use a number of techniques to help groups to distance themselves from conflict and rationalize and depersonalize challenges – reducing the emotions in play to enable clearer and more objective discussions, debates, and decisions to occur.

This is particularly important because, as Argyris and others highlight, under stress a group or individuals will often move from their "espoused" theory of action (what they say they think and do) to "theories in use" (what they actually think and do) which reflect their previous mental models and which are often unconscious, and "unilateral control models" (seeking dominance, not collaboration).

To help groups to escape from destructive conflict, the facilitator has three basic ways to intervene:

■ *Educating* – explaining what behaviors are productive and why in the context of facilitation.
■ *Role modeling* – demonstrating productive behaviors.
■ *Calling to account* – challenging unproductive behaviors.

Often, these types of interventions are used by facilitators in this sequence, for example:

■ Explicitly defining ground rules at the start of an event is "educating."
■ Participating in the group – asking clarifying questions and summarizing individual contributions – is "role modeling."
■ Challenging repeated disruptive behavior by individuals is "calling to account."

### Exploring difficult behavior that promotes destructive conflict
Deciding how and when to intervene with a group is a very personal judgment, usually driven by our preferences and past experience. Outlining theories about how to intervene is easy – but judging when to apply those intervention styles is somewhat harder.

The examples below show three classic participant behaviors for opposing change. No doubt you will recognize some of them.

---

### Mr. But

The group can never move on, because in every potential solution there is a hidden insurmountable problem that needs more consideration. There is always another detail needing to be considered. There is always another stakeholder who needs to be consulted before anything concrete can be agreed.

### Mrs. Impatient for Action

Everything is obvious, barely worth discussing – the answer is clear, what everyone needs to do is clear. Mrs. Impatient shuts down discussions, pushes the group to move on fast, and has a strong personal agenda – a conclusion and decision that she is impatient for the group to reach.

In weaker participants, she creates false consensus – unwilling to speak out and fight for deeper discussion, they acquiesce and then later fail to support her agenda. With stronger participants, she may feel attacked by their challenges to her views – and respond with impatience and condescension. The fights that ensue can be quite entertaining.

### Mr. Hand Grenade

Just as the group reaches an important decision or consensus, Mr. Hand Grenade reveals an issue that only he knows about such as "but the CEO has told the analysts that we're making no more IT investments."

Not only does this frustrate the group (and the facilitator), forcing the facilitator to rework ideas, it also demoralizes the group – making it feel powerless and less confident, destroying all its newfound optimism and confidence that it can really create change.

---

### Deciding when and how to intervene

A simple, fast method for determining an answer to "How destructive is this conflict?" is to assess how the conflict is perceived from two perspectives:

■ As facilitator or change leader, how strong do you think is the *necessity* to intervene to protect group effectiveness? In other words, how strongly do you believe that, if the conflict is not resolved, the group will not be able to produce a solution meeting the needs and standards of its stakeholders?
■ From the group's point of view, how actively are participants seeking and giving *permission* for intervention to redirect the conflict?

Mapping these answers together enables the facilitator to put the conflict in context, decide whether intervention is called for, and choose an appropriate type of intervention. Figure 3.2 below shows how this works – the answers to these questions shaping the appropriate type of facilitator intervention.

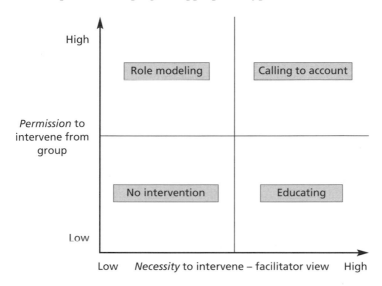

FIGURE 3.2 Deciding when and how to intervene in group conflict

The facilitator intervention depends on his or her perception of the need for intervention and the permission to intervene received from the group:

- *Calling to account* – explicitly challenging group members' unproductive behaviors – is usually only appropriate when the facilitator perceives a strong need to intervene and the group indicates clear permission or desire for this to happen.
- *Role modeling* productive behaviors for the group is most appropriate when the facilitator perceives little need to intervene but the group indicates a clear desire for them to do so.
- *Educating* – explaining what behaviors are productive and why – is often useful when the facilitator perceives a strong need to intervene but the group permission is less clear.
- *No intervention* is appropriate when the facilitator perceives little need to intervene and the group indicates little permission or desire for them to do so.

These are not, of course, definitive principles for intervention types. And there are a wide variety of circumstances which can affect and change the choices of an appropriate intervention style.

To know how and when to intervene, the facilitator must also diagnose the group's stage of development. As discussed in Section 2, this also drives the kind of intervention required – depending on whether the group is forming, storming, norming or performing, different interventions by the facilitator will be appropriate. An established group can "handle" individuals being called to account for behavior which does not support group effectiveness, whereas role modeling of behavior can be a less direct and more appropriate way of challenging behavior which does not support group effectiveness in a new group still in the process of forming.

Many group participants are frequent and experienced participants in groupwork and group conflict and therefore have strong views about conflicts. After all, most complex facilitated interventions are done with experienced managers with the organizational experience and status to affect change. So the group will often have articulate views about the sources and causes of its conflicts and why they may be more destructive than productive in conflict. Additionally, the group may have views about the stage of development it is at, and the relative influence of this upon its effectiveness in handling conflict. Listening to this informed insight from group members is essential to choosing the most appropriate intervention to defuse destructive conflict.

### *"Educating" to maintain group process effectiveness*

Explaining what behaviors are productive and why in the context of facilitation enables the group to rationalize and consciously decide to behave in ways that support group effectiveness in framing and conflict.

Establishing ground rules and explaining agendas are examples of the simplest forms of educating.

At a second level, education about the task and topic can be used to help a group to draw back from destructive conflict. Some sources of education include:

- Use of analysis tools to inquire into and explore opinions and values.
- Inviting experts, either from inside or outside the company.
- Visiting other firms in similar situations, customers and/or suppliers.
- Reviewing literature on the topic, articles from journals, case studies from business schools and corporate records (maybe the same problem was creatively addressed two or three years ago).

### *Examples of educating – intervening with Mrs. Impatient for Action*

With Mrs. Impatient for Action, educating is often the first response. Put the behavior on the table for discussion. Encourage the group and individual to question whether jumping ahead is useful behavior. Reinforce the power of inquiry and advocacy when used appropriately.

### *"Role modeling" – demonstrating productive behaviors*

Role modeling occurs when the facilitator temporarily becomes a participant in the group in order to set a standard of behavior. Facilitators can, and should, role model three distinct types of behaviors:

- "Responsible participation" (turning up on time, showing a level of respect for the process and other participants and stakeholders).
- Inquiry – asking open questions, exploring listening.
- Clarifying the advocacy of others – summarizing and confirming their positions and views.

---

### Balancing listening and intervention

One of the key skills for a facilitator in defusing destructive conflict is intervening to role model good inquiry and advocacy. As such, the challenge is to listen and summarize well. To do this requires a practiced approach to asking good questions (for example, asking a participant open questions such as "What do you think about the new product portfolio analysis?" as opposed to a closed question such as "Do you find the new product portfolio analysis useful?") It also requires an ability to intervene concisely so that the facilitator does not lecture the group and instead only "steers" them quickly and firmly back toward productive behavior.

Listening is an underrated skill. Consider what happens when we listen to children. They talk, express themselves, and get excited by the interest we are showing them. Participants will also do this if they feel that they are being listened to.

The use of a technique called "summarizing" is also very powerful. Again, consider what happens with a child – this time, one who is too young to express his or her own needs and wishes. An adult might say, "Do you want the ball?" If this summarizes the child's needs well, he or she will be excited and pleased. If not, shouting, crying or, at worst, tantrums will ensue. Summarizing what a participant says will make them think, "Yes, they have got it!" It also ensures that other group members understand too.

---

### *Examples of role modeling – intervening with Mr. But*

With Mr. But, role modeling is often the first response. If the group member is causing frustration, often you only need to give the group "permission" to challenge this behavior by role modeling inquiry in response to Mr. But's pessimism – asking repeatedly and patiently why Mr. But is expressing each doubt, seeking the root cause or belief behind his gloomy outlook.

Mr. But often jumps to advocacy too soon ("that won't work/doesn't matter and so on"). In this case explicit encouragement to suspend judgment may be required.

### "Calling to account" – challenging unproductive behaviors

Groups and individuals can often handle hearing more direct feedback than we expect. Our human instincts to avoid, rather than resolve, conflict cause us to be cautious in challenging individuals and groups to change their behaviors. And this caution is useful – an intervention seen as aggressive can severely reduce the facilitator's authority and influence on the group.

Calling to account is a strong form of feedback – individual or group behaviors are openly challenged and the reasons behind those behaviors explored.

### *Examples of calling to account – intervening with Mr. Hand Grenade*

With Mr. Hand Grenade, forceful challenge is required – call him to account. The "hand grenade" is an aggressive and explicit attempt to sabotage the group. There is only one appropriate response to this behavior. Direct challenge. Most probably, the sabotage raises an issue that needed addressing anyway and the tactic has only wasted time

The challenge for the facilitator, however, is to minimize the negative impact of this event on the group and the process. To do so we recommend a tactic of robust engagement and inquiry. Ask questions such as: "Why did you not tell us this earlier?" Use the event to explore why the emerging change is so strongly opposed.

The choice of approach for dealing with difficult participants is heavily dependent on the individual, the group, and the facilitator's own personal style. The guidance given here can only raise some of the underlying issues that should be considered in making that choice.

Overall, facilitators should guide their choice of tactics by asking themselves the question: What approach has the best chance of not provoking personal conflict and retaining or increasing the enrolment of the "difficult" individual and the wider group in the facilitation process – and the change process as a whole?

## Closing the event well – key deliverables to create momentum for implementation

Just as starting well required a great deal of preparation, there is also a good deal of work that the facilitator has to do to close the event well, both during and after the event.

The foundation for successful implementation is laid when the group is in the process of making decisions during a facilitated event. As such, there are several key deliverables that change leaders should expect in most circumstances from most facilitators:

- *Develop an implementation map* – at a minimum, the group must articulate the conclusions and agreements and confirm the commitment to change by designing a high-level action plan which outlines next steps and follow-up.
- *Agree a stakeholder engagement plan* – again, this may be possible only at high level, but without a commitment to engagement, the group will not take on the important task of building support and acceptance of change.
- *Review of the event* – to ensure that expectations have been met and learning from the event occurs.

A skilled facilitator will complete these tasks during the event so that the closing is a summary of what has already been said and agreed to. There should be *no* surprises and no attempts to close off unresolved issues during the conclusion of an event.

An effective conclusion is absolutely critical to a successful event but it is also the activity most likely to be neglected because earlier timing has slipped. Apply the following guidelines in order to ensure adequate time for a good finish:

- Overestimate the time required to close the meeting.
- Overestimate the time required to agree on actions and next steps.
- Plan opportunities to *repeat* final commitments and action plans – to confirm/consolidate them with the group.

The facilitator should also involve group members in ongoing time management decisions – they can lose ownership of outcomes if the facilitator changes the process too much without consulting them. This is particularly important in relation to issues which are unresolved. To ensure group ownership of the process, it is essential that *during* the event the facilitator highlights those issues that are being left unresolved and ensures explicit agreement within the group about how those issues will be resolved going forward.

## Closing an event well – the change leader's role

As a change leader, there are three important things you must do to ensure the group finishes its task well and sets a strong foundation for successful implementation:

■ *Meet the group and hear their recommendations* (if not present during the event): After the physical, mental and emotional hard work of creating new solutions to difficult problems, the group needs to voice its solutions to you, the change leader. Emailing a report or delegating one or two people to meet with you a week later demoralizes the group and sends it a signal that its work is of little importance.

■ *Listen to the group's reasoning and wider discoveries:* The group's solution is important. But more valuable to hear are the rationales behind its recommendations and the deeper understanding of the business that it has built during its work. It is those different ways of thinking about the business, those altered priorities, that will support, sustain, and expand change in the business – particularly if members of the group are senior and have wide authority. As change leader you need to signal the importance of this – and check out that you agree with them!

■ *Celebrate the group's success:* Do not only question and criticize. Express appreciation of the group's work and recognize its achievements and insights. If group members doubt your belief in their recommendations, they will doubt your commitment to support them in implementing change in the face of organizational opposition and inertia.

## Finishing on a high

Momentum for change is a fragile thing. The emotions felt by the group members as they leave an event will directly impact the success of the change initiative. Therefore it is essential that groups – and if possible change leaders and other stakeholders – "finish on a high." What does "finishing on a high" mean? No doubt you will have personal memories of it – it is completing a piece of work with a sense of progress, achievement, and optimism for the future. But what creates that feeling? Concrete progress, completion of key tasks, and a clear path forward. Thus for a group to "finish on a high," the facilitator must close the event well – the group must reach its objective for the event, participants must leave with a strong shared understanding of the new solution they have produced, the way it will be implemented, and clear credible short-term tasks and milestones to take their planned changes forward.

# Ensuring post-event follow-up and implementation

While the previous section focused on guiding and delivering a facilitated event, this section centers on ensuring that the change which has been proposed in the course of the event actually occurs and is implemented and embedded within the organization. It shows what facilitators and the change leader must do to maintain the momentum for change and ensure that decisions are translated into action. To do this, we will focus on four key points:

- Learning from the facilitation event.
- Overcoming common hurdles to implementation.
- Developing an implementation map.
- Rolling out the implementation map.

## Learning from the facilitated event

To fully assess the impact of a facilitated event, change leaders, participants, and facilitators need to take a step back and reflect upon it. This relection is of value to the change leader because it will not only lead to learning to improve future events but it can also positively affect the effectiveness of the group, particularly if it will also be responsible for the change implementation. Generally, evaluation of events can take place at four levels:

1. An immediate emotional reaction to an event.
2. Learning from the event.
3. Change of behavior as a result of the event.
4. Improved results.

With any strategic change event, we ultimately want to reach the fourth level, but we need to start with the event itself.

### Evaluating the immediate reactions to the event

Any good facilitator will conduct an informal, personal review of what worked and what did not in the facilitation design and delivery process to improve their future contribution to groupwork. This is all very well at a personal level, yet not sufficient for the group or change leader to ensure the implementation of change.

Valuable insights can be gained by involving participants and the change leader in a more extensive review. In many organizations, events are evaluated using "customer satisfaction" or "happiness" scales to assess immediate reaction. Many events use written evaluations with questions like: "How

| Excellent | Good | Fair | Poor | Very poor |
|-----------|------|------|------|-----------|
| (5) | (4) | (3) | (2) | (1) |

would you rate the value of this event to you?" or "How would you rate the value of the following events covered during the event?"

The most commonly used dimensions for evaluating events are:

1. Relevance of the design to the issues under discussion.
2. Process used to arrive at the outcome.
3. Quality of the outcome.
4. The group's commitment and confidence in implementing the agreed-upon changes.

Immediate reaction to the event is frequently used to assess whether this event should be repeated and if so whether it needs to be modified and whether the facilitator did a good job. But this is only the first level of evaluation: it has been shown that although participants who are interested or emotionally engaged in an event tend to retain more key pieces of information, this does not necessarily lead to behavioral change.

Actively involving the participants in the immediate post-event evaluation (not just getting them to fill out a questionnaire) makes the process more effective, as it can explicitly link group behaviors that occurred during the event to potential post-event situations. It can also be used as a vehicle for transferring ownership of the change process from the facilitator and change leader to participants – especially if the group is going to continue to work on the implementation of the solution moving forward. It also reinforces the message that the group's feedback on the process and content is valued.

## Learning from the event by debriefing

Debriefing involves reviewing the outcomes, processes, and interactions of the facilitated event to generate lessons learned. The value of debriefing lies in thinking about the mental links that lead to an outcome. Voicing these connections out loud moves the learning from implicit to explicit knowledge. This explicit knowledge is then much more readily applicable to new or similar situations. It helps to state "This is what I learned." But it also helps to identify what facilitated the learning, what made success and failure happen. And it helps to state "This is how I learned it."

It can happen at multiple levels: debriefing of individual behaviors, debriefing of the group dynamics and debriefing about the wider organizational implications which result from the discussions among the facilitated group. All these are essential if you, the change leader, are to learn from the event.

### Individual debriefing

In some facilitation processes, an "individual behavioral change" element is deliberately included. Whether it is formally included in the design or not, supportive or destructive individual behaviors are often identified during facilitation processes – simply because intensive groupwork provides a more transparent environment in which to observe individuals working together in groups. As a result, evaluation of individual group members inevitably occurs. The only key question becomes *how* that evaluation should occur – who should do it and who it should be shared with. At the simplest level, where people development is a low priority relative to task progress, evaluation can take the form of informal individual self-evaluation or informal peer feedback. In such situations, evaluation is implicit. When we were working recently to improve an organization's learning and knowledge management system, task achievement was the sole focus. So the change sponsor decided that individual feedback would be given only if it was sought by group members.

In other circumstances, evaluation of individual behaviors can be more explicit and more formal. In a project working to improve coordination of product development processes for a major food group, developing the strategy design and implementation skills of the group was an important secondary objective, so formal one-to-one feedback was planned – and the group was told before the event that this would happen. In these circumstances, the facilitator should properly and fully explain to participants how the evaluation information will be gathered and used. Transparency of the evaluation process does not always require transparency of evaluation content. Participants will typically accept, for example, that a facilitator may be expected to give feedback about individual group members to the change leader, but that they themselves will not be given free access to that data. If you, as leader of the change initiative, want improved results based on behavioral changes, then monitoring individual behaviors becomes an important part of post-event follow-up. One way to address this is to make these behavioral changes part of the individual objectives of the performance management system, so increasing the likelihood that the desired changes will actually materialize.

### Group debriefing

Debriefing a group by reviewing their interactions after the event leads to lessons learned as it involves revisiting the process and the actions taken and thereby establishes mental links between what was done and the outcome. This can then lead to a change in behavior or better problem-solving in the future. Ultimately it empowers the group to learn and create change (especially if the facilitated group is responsible for the implementation of decisions). But reviewing past activities is sadly not something that is commonly done among managers. Debriefing requires group members to discuss what they learned from their experiences that could be reapplied. It is a formal process where all the group members present during an event gather and review what happened, asking themselves difficult questions such as:

- What was the intent?
- What actually happened?
- Why did it happen?
- What did you think went well? And less well?
- What are the lessons learned?

### Learning by a senior management team

During a facilitated event, a business unit management team was investigating how to improve global launches of new products. It decided to conduct an after action review (AAR) on the recent successful launch of a nutritionally improved infant food. Having done so, it recommended that for all subsequent product launches, one project manager should be appointed to integrate all the separate activities that contribute to the launch, that is, R&D, operations, supply chain, marketing, sales, and logistics. This person would also be responsible for coordinating across markets so that the product could be launched in a number of geographic locations at the same time. As a result of the debriefing of past actions during a facilitated event, the team was able to reach decisions about what to do differently when moving forward.

At the end of a debriefing session, the group may have established a shared view of what worked and may therefore function better as a group in the future. Reflection about behaviors that were implicit in the group dynamics may have been openly addressed and the next time the group may be able to move forward faster.

Ideally, debriefing should focus on reviewing group dynamics. This can be done by the group on its own, with the presence of the change leader or even the facilitator. The group should identify telling incidents that were shining examples of good practice as well as incidences where it felt that issues were not resolved. If done by the leader of the group (if identified) or change leader, the role is one of facilitator. In many cases, this can be difficult for either the group leader or change leader as he or she is under pressure to model the type of behavior that he or she wants to see from the rest of the group. So from this point of view, he or she cannot dominate the discussion and has to be the first to admit that the group made mistakes. Because of the double role that the group leader needs to play, some groups sensibly choose to continue to work with the outside facilitator, who can help to guide the group through a structured discussion and make sure that it stays on track. A facilitator also helps to maintain a balanced discussion where all the participants can contribute and, through tough questioning, assists the group to tease out key lessons.

But ultimately, the group may want to take ownership of a debriefing process, as learning is more of a mindset than just a one-off event. In order for debriefing to become a routine, ownership of the process becomes a necessity. Managers need to have an open mind and the genuine desire to perform better. Going through the process takes a certain amount of humility and to begin with it may feel embarrassing to hear your faults being discussed, but with time it will become second nature. If debriefing is conducted in an environment that does not assign blame, then managers can feel safe voicing their opinions and admitting that they are less than perfect. And by learning not to immediately judge people but to understand how issues arose, we create an environment in which people are more likely to be innovative. With practice, analyzing success and failure can become a good habit. The group may, however, want to continue to use an outside facilitator.

### Debriefing on wider organizational issues

During an event, organizational issues that cause problems and inefficiency and which people in the organization currently "work around" are highlighted. At the end of an event or even post-event, there is the opportunity for the group to provide feedback to the change leader about "things that are not working" or "behaviors that are inconsistent." For example, when one group we worked with had identified some roadblocks to change, the executives noticed that part of the problem was that, despite the fact that entering Asia was stated as being an important strategic move, almost none of them ever spent time traveling to Asia.

When a group has identified issues that hinder the implementation of the plan, then facilitators, change leaders, and participants have to make a series of evaluations:

- How far will the perceived organizational problems limit the change event developed by the group?
- Based on that assessment, should specific organizational problems be in scope or out of scope within the change initiative?
- How widely should specific organizational problems be highlighted and how aggressively should solutions be sought?

Frequently a decision has to be made about the need to resolve wider organizational roadblocks before the group can actually implement the change plan. Three criteria should be used in making that decision:

■ The importance of the issue, based on how far it will affect the group's ability to achieve its change priorities.

■ The cost–benefit of resolving the issue – based on the complexity of the issue and the opportunity costs of investing organizational resources and effort in resolving it.

■ How far acknowledging and championing the issue by the change leader is necessary to ensure continued buy-in to the change process from key participants – ignoring or side-lining such an issue based on the first two criteria could risk causing key stakeholders to disengage from support of the overall change initiative.

The leader of the change initiative is required to make a judgment call with the group about the potential roadblock of the wider organizational issues that were identified by the group. If these roadblocks need to be removed, involving more executives may be necessary.

## Behavioral evaluation moves beyond reactions

As facilitated events are expected to lead to behavioral changes that will ultimately drive improved performance, it is important, several weeks or months after the event, to assess whether the changes have taken place.

We worked with a fast-moving consumer goods company which had conducted a number of facilitated events on implementing customer relationship management (CRM). Significant investments had been made to develop a large group of middle managers. After the events most of the managers were able to list the priority customers and point out what these customers wanted, but only a few actually worked with customers in a different way. Many of the managers had enjoyed the events but few applied the learning to the job. What went wrong? Apparently, there was little transfer of learning to behavioral change because the benefits of working differently with customers were understood intellectually but not emotionally and therefore actual behaviors did not change. In sum, little was done to move beyond intellectual understanding to emotional commitment in order to support new behaviors. Only when the group members had seen the benefits of this new approach to CRM in practice were they becoming emotionally committed. This level of emotional commitment may not happen in one facilitated event but over the course of time.

Follow-up on learning to ensure that it will lead to behavioral changes is key if a facilitated event is ultimately to impact performance. The role of the change leader is to put in place regular opportunities for evaluation. This can be done informally, by pointing out specific behaviors that clash with the newly defined norms, or formally, by including the behavioral expectations into a performance management system.

But however important evaluation may be, any change leader is ultimately interested in the outcome of the event.

## Improved results are the acid test

When has a facilitated event been a success? Purely and simply, when it leads to improved performance. Yet, publications point out that change initiatives are rated mostly or fully successful in around 30% of cases.[21] So the key questions are: What is going on? How can we improve the post-event success rate of change initiatives?

The change leader plays a key role in ensuring that the plans developed during a facilitation event will actually be implemented, because he or she is the one who can make that implementation a priority. To a great degree, it is the change leader's duty to work with the facilitator, other stakeholders, and the group before and after the event in order to ensure that as many as possible of the potential blockages to change are removed. Falling into the trap of a lack of follow-through may be the biggest barrier to improved performance.

## Recognizing and overcoming barriers to implementation[22]

There are many reasons why great decisions made in a facilitation event may not be successfully implemented. One of the most common is that, without realizing it, groups create formidable barriers in their ability to execute through the way in which they work together. Barriers to implementation are symptoms of a poor implementation culture among the group and the wider organization – the bad habits that undermine a group's ability to effectively implement its change plan. Maybe you will recognize some of them? Most organizations encounter these barriers at one time or another:

- Lack of clarity – being unclear on what needs to be done by the group.
- Lack of discipline – not living up to the group commitments.
- Lack of accountability – not knowing who will be accountable and not being prepared to get personally involved.

## Lack of clarity

The biggest barrier to implementation is lack of clarity. After all, if it is not clear what needs to be done, then it is hardly a surprise to find out that, whatever it was, it was not accomplished. If at the end of a facilitated event, it is not clear what decisions have been made, then the group will have the feeling that anything would fly.

Sometimes the problem is not a lack of decisions, but the fact that the decisions are ambiguous. When this happens, every person in the group constructs his or her own version of what needs to be prioritized. Even if the group has developed a change plan, it may not be crisp or tangible enough to be communicated downwards within the organization. A group participating in an event therefore not only needs to ensure that the decisions it makes are clear, it must also establish clear messages to communicate. This starts during an event, when the group needs to deal with conflicts, develop shared mental models, and document a decision once it has been made. But the need to resolve conflicts and reach decisions based on common frameworks continues throughout the entire implementation process.

In some cases, the group that participated at the facilitated event is going to actually implement the decisions reached. In this case, the individuals are likely to become a more permanent group or team, expected to work together until the implementation has been a success. In other cases, the group was already an intact team and the responsibility for implementation was clear to start with. In yet other cases, the group will dissolve upon completion of the facilitated event and either individuals within the group or others in the organization will be expected to implement the decisions. These are three very different situations and it is the role of the change leader to create clarity around the expected role of the group moving forward.

Here are some key questions that the change leader has to ask at the end of a facilitated event:

- What is the quality of decision reached by the group?
- Will it resolve the problem identified?
- Are the decisions clear and unambiguous?
- Are organizational stakeholders ready to hear the proposed change plans?
- How actively will you, the change leader, be involved in reviewing the results of the event with the group (if you were not present)?
- What role will you play in sharing the outcome of the facilitation event?
- Who is responsible for leading the implementation? Is it the group that developed the solution or others?

To ensure that the decisions reached and outcomes developed during the facilitation event will have an impact on the organization, the change leader needs to take responsibility for following up.

## Lack of discipline

Even if the group has made clear decisions, implementation will not happen without the discipline to follow it through. This is perhaps the most insidious of the barriers to implementation, because it quietly undermines the decisions. Discipline involves establishing acceptable standards of behavior and then enforcing those standards. In some companies disciplined action is just not on the agenda. Once a course of action has been decided, there appears to be no necessity for managers to follow it through. An agreement given to the boss is followed by a conscious decision to ignore anything that does not fit with one's own agenda or further one's power base within the organization. In some cases decisions are re-edited, readapted and reinvented to such an extent that the original directions are unrecognizable and incompatible with what the rest of the company is doing. Of course the most frequent reason that lack of discipline becomes an endemic part of the culture is that there are no consequences: no consequences for not following the path agreed on; no consequences for actively undermining colleagues; no consequences for a consistent lack of results. When pressed, managers often confess that they do not like follow-up. After all, starting up new change events is so much more fun, exciting, and glamorous than following up on the ideas that were agreed yesterday. Employees sense that if there is no follow-up, then the required actions were probably not all that important after all. Lack of discipline quickly permeates all levels of the organization. The key questions to the change leader are:

- How high on my agenda is follow-up of the decisions reached going to be?
- Will I be monitoring the results?
- Will I be participating at follow-up events if necessary?

## Lack of accountability

In some companies groups are not sure who will be accountable for post-facilitation events and, specifically, if the issue of accountability has not been discussed, groups may demonstrate a lack of personal commitment to the facilitation outcome and its success. Individually, they don't seem to want to get too involved. This can manifest itself in many ways. For some individuals it is just never their fault when something goes wrong. There are always a million reasons why implementation failed: the dollar, the head-quarters, the stupid customers, the competition, and the incompetent group members. But none of the reasons has anything to do with their own behavior. Some group members may believe that it is the job of the leader to ensure the implementation of the plan. Often they are heard starting sentences with "If I was in charge of this business ... ." It is as if because they do not have total control, they should not be accountable for results at all. Many people do not realize that implementation will be a lot of hard work. In many large organizations there are places to hide, where if you play your cards right, people will not suspect that in fact you are not doing very much. Here again are a number of questions that you as change leader should ask yourself:

- How will individual members of the group be rewarded for their contribution?
- Will I ensure that they are rewarded?
- How high are the stakes for me?
- Will I provide feedback to individuals?

Lack of clarity, discipline, and accountability sound like formidable barriers, yet every organization is guilty at some time or another of fostering habits that do not encourage successful implementation of decisions. So what can we do to change the way in which we work to improve our bad habits?

## Developing an implementation map is necessary to ensure impact

Developing an implementation map or plan starts during the facilitation event but is an ongoing process that continues post-event. During the event, decisions may have been taken, but without an understanding of what their implementation will actually look like, the prospects for implementation are low. There are five specific steps[22] (illustrated in Figure 4.1) that need to be taken in order to overcome the three barriers to implementation and improve the chances that the decisions reached during the facilitated event will happen. They are:

1. Documenting the decisions made.
2. Developing action plans.
3. Getting buy-in from stakeholders.
4. Ensuring follow-up within the group.
5. Rewarding individuals for their contributions.

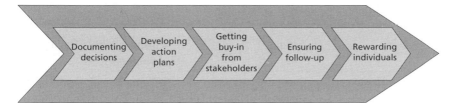

FIGURE 4.1 Implementation map

## Documenting the decisions

It seems like an obvious step, but many groups leave a facilitated event or post-event meeting without a written record of the decisions made or the plans agreed upon. This leaves "wriggle-room" for everyone involved who may want to avoid commitment. As discussed in Section 3, at the beginning of a facilitated event, it needs to be clear who will document the decisions made or action plans agreed upon. In some cases, it is the facilitator and in other cases a group member who will take on this responsibility. The advantage of the facilitator documenting the decisions is potential objectivity, leaving little room to reinterpret decisions when capturing them on a piece of paper. It does, however, distract the facilitator from the task of managing the process. The advantage of using a group member lies in the group taking ownership of the outcome. Whoever does the work, everyone needs to be able to walk away with a written document. This also applies to routine meetings the group will use to follow through. Ensure that decisions made at these meetings will be documented.

## Developing action plans

Assuming that the group will continue to work together after the facilitated event, it is important to ensure that the event is closed with everyone "on the same page" about what they are expected to do. The key question to answer is: How will we work together in terms of our actions and behaviors to implement the change plan? Ideally, a group agenda should be developed, outlining the initiatives that were discussed and identifying action plans for each one. This can be followed by the group deciding on ground rules for continued work together beyond the facilitated event: How will each person contribute and how will they support the group? At the end, each group member should be able to walk away with a clear list of action items as well as an understanding of how they will be supported by other group members. Simple Gantt charts can help summarize the actions decided.

TABLE 4.1 Example post-event action plan

| Objectives | Actions | Responsibility (who/dept) | Timing |
|---|---|---|---|
| Understand customer needs | Undertake customer studies in all target markets | AV (marketing) | April 1 2007 |
| Understand how to best position ourselves versus competing companies, their products, and strategies | Identify key competitors, their strategies, product portfolios, key channels, target market, and strategies | GH (planning) | May 15 2007 |

Make sure that a name and a date are connected to each of the items. This will ensure accountability for every group member. To establish clear expectations of each other, they need to consider reviewing a few key questions such as:

- Are individual responsibilities clear and known by all in the group?
- Are deliverables and measurable objectives from each of us clear and known by all in the group?
- Will we coordinate directly with each other?
- Will we ensure that there is open communication?
- Will we conduct regular feedback between each other?
- Do we have an agreed-upon, common agenda for groupwork and the purpose it must serve?

Revisiting expectations about how the group will continue to work with each other ensures ongoing accountability after the event has finished. Action plans also ensure that each group member is accountable for the tasks he or she has to accomplish.

## Getting buy-in from stakeholders

Many groups think that, having developed an action plan, they are ready to execute it. To a lesser or greater extent, they will, however, need to enlist stakeholders both inside and also, potentially, outside the organization. For some change plans, you may only need the limited involvement of certain people from the organization who will work alongside the group at various points in time. But if the plan is likely to have far-reaching consequences across the organization, you may need to engage and communicate with many more people. For instance, the decision to use customer segmentation in marketing may have far-reaching consequences, and you may need the support of the financial director and the distribution director as well as the marketing department.

Getting people involved will take time and energy and must not be done haphazardly. You cannot just hope that people will immediately commit to supporting the group and that they will magically know how they can assist, or even that they will want to. Many of them will know nothing about what you are trying to do or why it is so important. To make sure that you get the right people involved and committed, the group needs to create a stakeholder engagement plan. This could be done during the facilitated event or post-event.

### Barriers to buy-in

There are *three potential barriers* to getting buy-in that ought to be avoided when developing an implementation map:

1. Change is imposed by the leader.
2. Stakeholder involvement is too narrow.
3. The mindset is about control and domination.

### Change is imposed by the leader

In many organizations, change is designed by a top management team with the assumption that people will be against it and will therefore need to be told to make it happen. In order to avoid resistance or sabotage, the designers of the change often seek compliance only to find out that the more they do so, the more those who are supposed to be implementing the change will do their own thing, or do nothing, which often results in the failure of the entire change initiative.

To avoid this, you need to involve all those who have a major influence on the outcome. They need to realize for themselves that change is necessary, and that they need to adapt their mental models. Sabotage or resistance frequently occurs as a result of differences in mental models. In order to move to a higher degree of "sharedness" in mental models, individuals need to notice the gap between current reality and the shared vision. Helping individuals to acknowledge the existence of this gap is the first step. The next is to create strategies and action plans together, with each person taking responsibility for the successful implementation of these plans or their part of them. This makes large group interventions or follow-up meetings a necessity.

We worked with a group in the food industry that had just hired a new CEO. In the course of a week-long facilitated event, the group decided on 10 strategic priorities and action plans for each one. Once they had a shared sense of implementation plans which outlined the required change, it was time to share their intentions with the rest of the organization, so two weeks after the facilitated event, this senior group invited 400 managers from around the world to a two-day event to get their buy-in. The senior group and the invited managers jointly revisited the action plans developed by the senior group during the facilitated event and made minor adaptations to ensure that the plans got buy-in from those who had to execute them.

### Stakeholder involvement is too narrow

We mentioned that considering stakeholders is an important part of the design of any event. This is because they may be people with a great deal of influence and it is foolish to ignore their opinions. It also means that, by ignoring key stakeholders, the group planning the change is ignoring some of the current reality and therefore has only an incomplete picture of the starting conditions. As a result, the group may make strategic decisions with, at best, limited information.

The more widely we are able to establish acceptance of the necessity for change and the type of change it is likely to be, the greater the chances of it being implemented. However compelling the vision of change may be, the people who are most likely to take full ownership of the outcome are those who feel involved. Again, this makes large group follow-up a necessity.

### Control and domination is the mindset

Given the frequently unpredictable nature of change and the associated threat of its unwanted consequences, many leaders feel that they need to control the process in the greatest detail and leave little room for groups to develop their own ideas. Micromanagement becomes the name of the game. In these situations, the group has little space to make adaptations to a predestined path.

Before a group starts engaging in a facilitated event and even after a map for implementation has been developed, dialog between the change leader and the group is necessary in order to find the right balance between ownership by the group and ensuring that the strategic direction set by the change leader will be kept in mind. To ensure accountability, the change leader may also want the group to own the action plans developed, despite the fact that there are constraints that may require some control.

To ensure that the decisions reached during the event stand the highest chance of succeeding, there needs to be a two-way contract between the group and the change leader. Firstly, the change leader needs to confirm that the decisions truly will lead to performance improvement once implemented and, secondly, the change leader needs to be satisfied with the implementation map and therefore willing to provide the support the group needs in order to execute it.

Creating commitment frequently goes beyond the change leader and requires dialog between the group and wider organizational stakeholders; this typically takes place over the course of several meetings. The underlying assumption is that by involving more people and getting their inputs, more creative and potentially acceptable programs of change are developed, which, with wider support, stand a higher chance of being implemented successfully.

### Map stakeholders to understand who needs to be engaged

Conducting a stakeholder analysis to assess the key people and departments affected by the decisions to be implemented is the starting point for engaging those who did not participate in the facilitation event. The ultimate goal is to get an understanding of those people who can make an impact within the organization. While some are influential, for example opinion leaders, others may have formal power but little influence in driving others to adopt their views. The degree of impact may not necessarily be linked to the formal hierarchy. Although formal power may help to get others moving, looking at the informal network is probably a more meaningful way to assess who the gatekeepers, innovators, and network leaders are. Table 4.2 shows a way to assess stakeholders.

Which key persons and departments are affected by the implementation of the decisions reached during the facilitated event, and in what capacity?

TABLE 4.2 **Stakeholder mapping**

| Who?<br>(key people or departments) | Importance to success<br>(5 = very important, 1 = not important at all |
|---|---|
|  |  |
|  |  |

The next step is to assess each of the critical stakeholders in terms of their level of agreement with the strategic initiative and their capabilities in contributing to the expected outcomes. Knowledge about their position and potential reaction to company decisions, and how they might interact with each other, affects the proposed decision's chances of success. In addition to knowing where the critical stakeholders stand, managers need to think about the skills and capabilities they need if they are to implement the strategic initiative. It does not help you much to have a committed individual who does not have the skills to implement. Figure 4.2[23] shows how you can assess where those who you have identified as critical stakeholders stand.

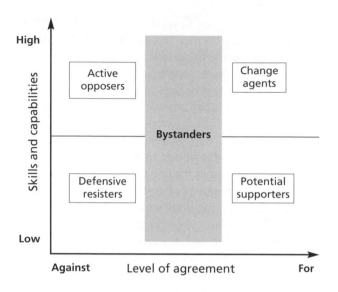

FIGURE 4.2 Stakeholder assessment map

In this example:

- The *change agents* are your ideal stakeholders: they both support the project's goals and proposed actions, and have the skills to help implement them. This group may include clients, end users or highfliers who see the strategy implementation as an opportunity to make their mark.
- *Potential* or *armchair supporters* agree with the strategic plan, but are less able to contribute. Outside the organization this group may include suppliers, consultants, and financial institutions; inside it could be other business unit managers who see the strategic plan as a testing ground, which does not affect them in the short term.
- *Neutral stakeholders* or the so-called *bystanders* are neither highly threatening nor especially collaborative. Although they may have a stake in the project and its decisions, they are generally not concerned about most issues. However, they should not be ignored, as a change in circumstances may shift them away from the sidelines to become either actively against or actively cooperative with the project: an environmental group, for example, might not feel that the project concerned it, until it became aware of the possible increase in pollution.
- *Defensive resisters* have a high potential to have a negative influence on the initiative but a low potential for collaboration. They can be one of the most distressing groups for a group in charge of implementation. Typical non-supportive stakeholders include competing organizations or individuals who have most to lose from the change.

■ *Active opposers* are typically individuals with different views about the strategic direction the company should take and can have a detrimental effect, but if they can be convinced of the value of the proposed change, they have the potential to contribute to its implementation, possibly even by refining it.

### Develop a stakeholder engagement plan

Once the critical stakeholders are identified, the next step is to develop a *stakeholder engagement plan* in dealing with them (see Table 4.3 below). Mobilizing stakeholders helps to overcome the resistance to change, which is a natural phenomenon. Getting stakeholders' commitment and successfully overcoming resistance to the implementation of decisions involving change are prerequisites for success. Each critical stakeholder group will need to be managed differently as their capacity to impact the change will vary. While some stakeholders are gatekeepers who control access to a critical resource such as IT, which provides access for intranet newsletters, or HR, which can organize training, others are opinion leaders who play a critical role in shaping people's views; a third group are network leaders who know everyone informally. For example, we recently worked with an oil company where we discovered that health and safety managers controlled a critical resource – approval to make any changes to operating procedures – whereas technical experts were the most important opinion leaders, influencing how changes would be accepted, and the general managers were in fact network leaders – most influential through their ability to coordinate communication with multiple stakeholders.

Based on the typology of different types of critical stakeholders, five strategies emerge for managing them. Initially, you will probably start with the change agents. You need to actively involve them in decisions related to the implementation. We argue that this collaboration must be based on mutual trust and must be beneficial for both parties. Giving the change agents responsibilities and decision-making power will increase their level of commitment and encourage them to convince others who may be opposed to the initiative. The potential supporters are often ignored as stakeholders to be managed, and therefore their cooperative potential may also be overlooked. This group should be developed, informed, and involved in issues which they have the skills to help implement. Bystanders who are potentially marginal stakeholders and whose potential both for affecting the implementation and for collaboration is low should simply be monitored in order to avoid negative surprises. Their "wait and see" attitude often makes them followers in a change process. Managers will probably want to minimize the time and effort they spend on this group, yet keep an eye on it in case decisions could impact some of its opinion leaders. Non-supportive stakeholders, particularly the defensive resisters, are initially best managed by using a defensive strategy.

This may mean showing individuals how the change best aligns with their skills. This can be difficult; therefore, others argue that non-supportive stakeholders are best managed by keeping them busy with other initiatives. Active opposers are probably the most distressing group for managers, as they have the skills and capabilities to sabotage the intended change. They may, however, have valid suggestions to make. Change agents may help to convert opposers and, if they are convinced, they could potentially become your biggest supporter; if not, a more radical approach may be necessary.

---

**Analyzing stakeholders and developing an engagement plan**

The CEO of a rapidly growing European consumer goods company charged a group of high potential managers to investigate how to differentiate the company's offer using its internet-based distribution channel. One option was to segment its market and to use this channel to increase customer loyalty in the different market segments. By doing this, the company was hoping to increase the efficiency with which it recruited and retained high-value customers. As this initiative had far-reaching consequences for the company, understanding who in the organization could contribute to it was of significant importance. So the group looked at groups of people within the organization who needed to be enrolled in the initiative as well as how to engage them. Following this analysis, the managers realized that to guarantee the successful launch of a segmented distribution approach they would have to do significant internal selling.

---

TABLE 4.3 Example stakeholder engagement plan

| Whom? | Proposed approach to engage stakeholder |
|---|---|
| CEO | Convince during initial presentation |
| IT | Explain added value to company and ask for additional resources |
| Internet team | Convince with vision: This will be the most creative website in the world |
| Internal marketing | Roll-out of a real customer segmentation as stepping stone for the future |
| Markets | Convince with presentation containing fact and figures |
| Commercial | Better understand new entry barriers for the competition and long-term added value |
| R&D | Help them to become a prime mover in innovation |
| PR | Help them to innovate in communications |

## Ensure that the change plan will be communicated

While the critical stakeholders may be the starting point, the potential for change recipients to block new plans should not be underestimated. Therefore a communication plan needs to be developed for everyone who has not already been reached. Most frequently, it is middle level managers who need to be motivated first. They influence lower level managers to act upon the strategic goals and if they are not on board the danger of sabotaging the action plan is at its highest. The effectiveness of communication relies on managers using communication processes and messages that are perceived as understandable and trustworthy, especially in the early stages of implementation. Using concise messages and clearly defined terms as well as precluding the suppression of truth or misstatements of expectations is part of an effective communication system. There should be no ambiguity regarding the difference between truthfulness and integrity in the messages and "looking good" for the sake of convincing others.

## Adapting messages for different audiences is key

Keeping in mind that effective communication requires adapting messages for different audiences, it is important to map out which stakeholders – both internal and external – need to be informed and about what. Some of the internal stakeholders could be middle management, different functional departments or employees. External stakeholders could include suppliers, customers, trade unions, and so on. To each group a different message may have to be sold, for example sharing the reasoning for the decision, the resource implications and how these decisions fit within the strategy. Effectively for each group, a sub-project can be identified which requires specification of who would lead communication, when and what media to use, goals to be achieved, resources needed, and follow-up required. This plan can also be developed during the facilitated event so that the group has a head start on implementation. When a senior executive from a large telecommunications company was presenting the largest ever undertaking of change to a critical group of middle managers, he made sure that he only focused on a limited number of key messages in his introductory five-minute speech. The audience clearly understood the reasons for the urgency of change as these few messages focused on creating that understanding.

## Ensure share of mind of the change plan and nurture knowledge

The goal of an overall communication action plan is to ensure that as many key people as possible understand and agree with the change plan. But, effective communication also supports and nurtures knowledge within the organization over time. Communicating the latest performance keeps individuals aware of the organization's current status. Especially when the communication needs to lead to action, encouraging the sharing of individuals' experiences creates sustained commitment to the action plan. This may best be accomplished by intense and frequent sharing, and by dialog rather than one-directional reporting. If communication is a one-off event, most change processes are doomed to fail. Communication must take place at regular intervals, informing different groups of progress, possibly leveraging other communication opportunities such as formally scheduled task force meetings, informal lunch conversations or coffee breaks.

Alignment and clear communication of shared goals will go a long way to breaking through the inevitable barriers to success. Letting managers know their role in overcoming functional barriers, such as their authority to free up resources and make quick decisions to address problems within their areas, will help to drive the change process. Aligning strategic goals with sub-unit performance and rewards will help to motivate managers as they can see the benefit for themselves. By communicating the performance expectations, ultimately the drivers of strategic goals, managers can channel the organization's energies, abilities, and specific knowledge toward achieving the business's goals. It is important to ensure that the group responsible for implementation agrees on the way forward, has a common story to tell, and can answer likely questions consistently before large-scale communication begins. Much of the thinking about this has hopefully been done during the facilitation event, but the larger the degree of change that emerges, the greater becomes the responsibility of the facilitator to bring to the group's attention the need to carefully plan out stakeholder engagement and communication.

## Ensuring follow-up within the group

Once stakeholders have been identified and communication messages drawn up, there is still the danger that there will be no follow-up. Before everyone leaves a facilitated event, accountability has to be clarified. In many cases, the same group that participated in the facilitation event will be responsible for implementation. In this case, group members will need to organize formal follow-up mechanisms: simply trusting that implementation will take place is not enough, as many individuals may have a double implementation agenda – a regular job that already keeps them busy and being a member of a group that is expected to implement a change initiative. If we are not careful, this double agenda can produce the perfect excuse not to make progress on the decisions reached. To stand any chance of success, formal mechanisms of follow-up need to be planned and organized. This is best done before implementation gets underway, so ideally it should be completed during the facilitated event. If not, it should be one of the first steps to be completed afterwards.

Formal follow-up can be planned in terms of post-event meetings. Scheduling them ahead of time is important as it reminds the group of the priority of the decisions and ensures that implementation is monitored. At the same time, it also makes sure that those who participated in the event will work efficiently as a group once the plan has to be executed. These planned meetings are the opportunity to ensure follow-up for the agreed-upon deliverables. Action plans decided upon during a facilitation event will become organizational reality if they reappear during regular operating meetings and if individual rewards are linked to them.

Creating a group agenda of actions to be regularly reviewed ensures that the agreed-upon plans will be discussed and decisions will be made about the next steps. It also ensures that implementing the change plan remains at the front of everyone's mind. This is then supported by scheduling a series of short meetings to be held on a regular basis and attended by all the core group members. The purpose is to create peer pressure from the group for everyone to attend and for each group member to deliver on the tasks they were assigned. Group members are more likely to take meetings seriously if they are, say, every Tuesday at 11, than if they are slotted in haphazardly to already full schedules. The regularity of the meetings helps the group to function effectively and becomes the "heartbeat" of the change project. Without regularity, the change plan is easily forgotten and put to one side in preference for business as usual. "Out of sight" rapidly becomes "out of mind."

In addition, we all know that badly run meetings waste valuable time and become a sink for group energy and enthusiasm. If the group that participated in the facilitation event continues to work together, it will probably already have ground rules about behaviors which it can use during follow-up meetings. Some examples of behaviors for the follow-up could be:

- We have an agreement that everyone will attend group meetings.
- We have rules for punctuality in delivering on promises and commitments, in responding to questions, and in following up.
- We have confirmed the regularity of face-to-face meetings as top priority.
- We require every group member to be prepared for meetings.
- During group meetings, we expect every group member to listen to others and to promote an "advocacy–inquiry" style.
- Interruptions during meetings are not acceptable (fines for phones ringing, for answering them, for leaving the room …).
- We make sure that decisions are restated at the end of meetings.

For each of these statements, you should discuss how you are doing as a group, using the examples provided, and possibly adding some more points that you think would be helpful (note that these examples are not an exhaustive list of "group musts" but a suggestion of what you may want to consider). These ground rules not only help the group to maintain discipline and ensure group effectiveness, but they also demonstrate accountability towards the change leader.

Documenting decisions, developing action plans, and scheduling follow-up are essential to ensure that the change plan evolved during a facilitated event will actually be implemented.

## Reward individuals for their contributions

While action plans ensure clarity on the tasks that group members are expected to undertake, when they need to be completed, and what they are expected to deliver, these objectives are frequently not measurable. In order to ensure delivery, objectives ought to be measurable using hard data and facts. When the individuals responsible for implementation have multiple responsibilities, personal objectives need to be aligned with those of group members and with areas where coordination is necessary. If action plans and responsibilities are not coordinated, confusion will reign once implementation gets underway. This is especially true when group members' work is incompatible with their other responsibilities. All group members need to understand what they are expected to contribute and then list all the tasks for which they will be held accountable. These tasks normally need to include information about the deliverables and the deadline for completion.

This may, however, not be enough. In addition to adding the group and personal objectives to the yearly performance objectives, there should be a mechanism in place through which the line manager receives feedback on group members' performance at the end of the year so that individuals can be rewarded.

Rewards may or may not be financial. Non-financial rewards can be more motivating than financial ones. The most important non-financial rewards are promotion within the organization and public recognition for a good job well done. Financial rewards should, however, not be overlooked. Although working on a change initiative may already be seen as a high-profile job and therefore get recognition, the individual concerned may not consider this sufficient unless it is accompanied by tangible benefits. At the same time, accountability of the individuals contributing is more likely to be ensured.

One change leader, talking about a recent project, told us: "My group members are supposed to dedicate 30% of their time to the initiative. But they are finding it very difficult to reduce their line function duties by this amount. So during the 'hot' phases, all group members worked at 130% and spent substantial amounts of their spare time during evenings and weekends on the initiative." And in the end the group was not very satisfied. Group members may not have expected a "big reward" but as one said: "I would at least appreciate a thank you."

## Engaging the wider organization with an implementation map post-facilitated event

Any facilitation event is part of a bigger change journey. Overcoming the barriers to implementation by developing an implementation map consisting of documented decisions, action plans, engagement plans for stakeholders, planned follow-up within the group, and individual rewards is the start for implementation, but further events may be necessary to ensure full buy-in and roll-out. In the process, adaptations to the change may be made by stakeholders.

Essentially, change leaders have multiple options to engage the wider organization. Using facilitated events with a small group of key decision-makers is just the beginning. Engaging stakeholders from the larger organization through interventions using facilitated or non-facilitated events is an important means of achieving buy-in. In some cases, the change leader may run the event together with his or her immediate subordinates without further facilitation. In other cases, he or she may decide to again use a facilitator (inside or outside) to engage other stakeholders. Getting buy-in and support from a larger number of stakeholders increases the chances of successful implementation of change and will lead to increased performance.

### Large group events help create buy-in

One way to ensure that you get buy-in from stakeholders outside the group that developed the change plan is to organize large group interventions – one or more interactive events flowing from a first facilitated event. Each gathering is attended by a large number of participants (10 to 2,000 or more), from all levels and functions of the organization, plus representatives from other key stakeholder groups (potentially outside the company). Together the participants address real issues of strategic importance and thereby enable the organization to move toward a shared vision of the future. The more you are able to get buy-in of the enlarged stakeholder group, the higher the chances of successful implementation of the agreed-upon change plan. As most facilitated events will only reach a limited number of people, there is a need to continually assess who within the organization needs to be engaged and through what means – another facilitated event, a meeting, training or other activities that will engage these stakeholders.

## A facilitated event among the leadership team was the start of creating change

In November 2005, a new head of Nestlé Nutrition was appointed. He inherited a newly created organization that was in the process of being separated from Nestlé's core business. From being a strategic business unit, Nestlé Nutrition was to become a business with full profit and loss responsibility, and was to be operational in January 2006.

The new head started working with his management team to establish the Nestlé Nutrition Strategic Blueprint – the document that would be the guiding light for reaching the required financial targets. He decided to organize a one-week facilitation event with his team in order to develop the strategic agenda in more detail and ensure that action plans would be developed, with individuals on the team accountable for the results. During the event, Must-Win Battles (MWBs)[24] were formulated that would represent the agenda for the Nestlé Nutrition central management team in the coming months. The battles were identified to support the markets in winning and delivering superior global performance. Of the 13 that were chosen, 10 focused on developing competencies; 3 were business-specific. One, for instance, focused on improving the understanding of customer needs, another on ensuring quality and safety of products.

### The roll-out of facilitated events across geographic regions created buy-in

This was, however, only the starting point of the strategic change. As Nestlé Nutrition was operating in countries across six continents – Europe, North and South America, Africa, Australia and Asia – the management team had to ensure that the newly developed Strategic Blueprint and its associated changes would be implemented, so a handbook for rolling out facilitated events within each of the geographic regions was developed. The handbook was designed as a reference tool to support the running of interactive workshops with Nestlé Nutrition employees in different geographic regions. At the end of each workshop, regional and national groups were expected to have:

- A clear understanding of their local MWBs.
- A clear definition of what success looks like.
- A clear action plan (including actions and accountabilities) to share with other groups via the Nestlé Nutrition intranet site.

For each country business group, there would be different, locally critical MWBs that would help to achieve global goals.

### Implementation was guaranteed by ensuring accountability around identified priority action plans

Developing MWBs in an interactive fashion has become the Nestlé Nutrition way of prioritizing efforts and energy around common targets. At the same time, they ensure accountability to defined priorities and because the results are shared they are a valuable tool, helping individuals to learn from each other and to reapply corporate knowledge and skills across the Nestlé Nutrition community. Awards were created to honor the best MWBs. In this way MWBs create value for both customers and shareholders.

To ensure implementation, the global management team also developed a "how to" document allowing regional groups to run locally organized facilitated events focused on developing MWBs to help reach their business goals. This is designed to help play a part in achieving the Nestlé Nutrition Strategic Blueprint. It defines four stages of the MWB process (Figure 4.3).

*Stage 1:* Defining the MWBs

*Stage 2:* Engaging people with the action plan

*Stage 3:* Driving performance and monitoring progress

*Stage 4:* Learning, sharing and reapplying our experiences

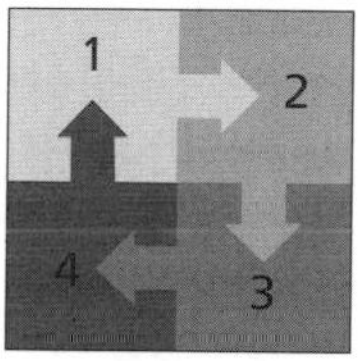

FIGURE 4.3  Four stages of the Must-Win Battle process

### Sharing experiences meant continued engagement

Developing MWBs interactively is strategy in action. MWBs essentially outline priorities. They are urgent and must be acted on quickly. The result is high levels of engagement and commitment. There is an opportunity to harness the considerable talent of people in the company by engaging their hearts and minds with the MWBs. Thereby sustained change with high performance can be achieved.

### By rolling out the strategic change plan to the larger organization, decisions made by key stakeholders can be partially adapted and thereby improved

In most cases, it is advisable to place constraints on the amount of adaptation that can be made when discussing the plans with a larger group, as there is always the danger that new groups will want to reinvent the wheel. At the same time, sufficient room needs to be provided so that when circumstances change, or new problems or information emerges, adaptations can be made. Once the change leader has sufficient buy-in from the affected stakeholders, implementation will be more successful. This does not, however, mean that changes will not become necessary at a later stage of implementation. Facilitated events may then be needed again in order to sustain the change. Ultimately, facilitation is effective when it leads to buy-in from key stakeholders and accountability on the part of individuals implementing the change. This is the key to creating lasting change that produces results.

## Facilitated events lead to shared mental models which is the starting point for any lasting change

Facilitated events can lead to lasting change as they enable individuals to revisit their "outdated" mental models of "why and how things work in our group and organization" and thereby not only lead to higher quality solutions of entrenched problems but also to a mental solution shared by all those participating in the event. For groups to accept that their mental models are outdated is the first step in change. Reaching a shared model of what the solution could be is the outcome of a facilitated event and is the second step. Both of these steps are the starting point for organizational change. They set the stage for the next two steps by building the urgency, energy, and commitment needed to take action and commit resources. Framing and productive conflicts, within these first two steps, are not a guarantee that change will be implemented or successful, but the absence of one or both is a strong predictor of failure.

Understanding the group and organizational context prior to an event increases the likelihood of taking the constraints into consideration and will therefore lead to a solution that the group is able to implement. Post-event follow-up initially consists of an assessment of the degree of urgency that exists within the organization to accept a new mental model and the readiness of stakeholders to commit to a new course of action. The more the solution developed by the facilitated group is a departure from the existing mental models within the organization, the less ready the organization is to accept change.

Follow-up then becomes necessary to overcome the barriers to change that re-emerge when the group working on the solution disperses. Follow-up is a more concrete, action-oriented, and increasingly labor-intensive step toward achieving change, but the chances for failure, errors, mishaps, second guessing, and other forms of discomfort all exist here with higher degrees of possibility and probability. Consequently, this is where groups require the most support. Any leader of change needs to see the broader context of a facilitated event as consisting of a timeline that starts with the planning, designing, guiding, and follow-up of events that may need to be repeated to create lasting change.

Over time, any leader of change initiatives will have to assess how ready the organization is for the developed solutions, and potentially make adjustments if the changes don't lead to the expected actions and outcomes. The speed of implementation will depend on the urgency with which the changes need to be made, given the performance of the business, as well as the willingness of members of the organization to accept the proposed changes. The higher the urgency and readiness for change, the more quickly any implementation is likely to occur. In situations of low urgency and low readiness, it is harder for change leaders to persuade the organization to develop a shared mental model of why and how to change. Often the change that could create most value within an organization is the change most actively resisted. In these cases, as an experienced change leader, you will know the necessity and pain of patience and perseverance. Often when change is hard, repeated facilitation interventions, ongoing communication plans, and continuing facilitator input to support implementation can be important tools to help you to embed your change agenda. It is in these cases that leaders may want to ask facilitators to help them to create a sense of urgency, by getting individuals to accept the fact that they have outdated mental models, and then building commitment among a key group of stakeholders by developing shared perceptions of the solutions that will lead to higher performance.

Since change is an ongoing process, the role of the facilitator may continue beyond an initial facilitated event. In many cases, the relationship between the change leader and facilitator will exist for an extended period of time to ensure that the implementation will not stop at one group of people. As there is the danger that successful change will lead to complacency over time, an eye needs to be kept on continuous improvement opportunities. As Figure 4.4 shows, facilitation is best used when there is a low perceived urgency for change and low organizational readiness. In this case, facilitated events are a key tool for any change leader.

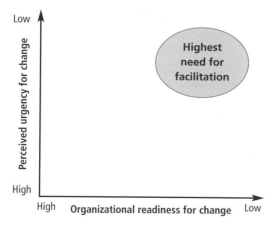

FIGURE 4.4 The impact of urgency and readiness for change on the need for facilitation

# APPENDIX 1

## Research findings

### Executive summary

We investigated process guidance and framing in order to understand their impact on the outcome of group facilitation interventions. Based on the analysis of 27 group facilitation interventions, we found that the value of group facilitation depends not only on process guidance but also on the provision of frameworks – but that these two factors were important for different types of outcomes. While process guidance is important in expanding the group's thinking and thereby changing mental models, providing frameworks is an important determinant in the perceived value of facilitation.

### Introduction

Managers and their groups face increasing pressures to modify strategies in order to improve performance. Yet, the modification of strategies involves strategic change that is difficult to achieve. To help companies develop and achieve this change, managers have employed different types of interventions within their business, one of which is group facilitation. Group facilitation is used in the context both of changing organizations and in business schools to help company groups to develop alternative courses of action and agree upon a plan forward. In the past, the use of facilitation has primarily been experiential, with limited research invested in understanding factors that impact the outcome.

The reason strategic change is difficult to achieve is that it requires a shift in mental models among the group embarking on the journey of change. Mental models can be defined as beliefs held by a group of people that precede behavior and actions. While a large number of different terms are used for mental models,[25] there is broad consensus among academics that they mediate between individual actions and external stimuli and are particularly important as mediators in cases of change.

Within organizations, individuals need to coordinate their actions in order to accomplish organizational goals. Individuals working together therefore need to develop shared mental models based on common values and beliefs which will be the basis for making decisions and taking action. While individual changes in beliefs are difficult to achieve, changes in collective beliefs are even more pervasive, because collective beliefs are embedded in routines and organizational practices that are learned over time. They are socially legitimized and act as barriers to change.

Perceiving the need for change requires a change in mental models. Failure to recognize this need limits options for action as alternatives erode. Recognizing the need for change frequently requires strong signals, which could involve conflict within the group or even a crisis. But the result is the starting point for considering alternative courses of action. Time then needs to be set aside for investigating these options. Facilitated group interventions serve the purpose of raising recognition among the people involved of the need for change.

## Facilitated group interventions

Facilitated interventions are an opportunity for groups to develop shared mental models by integrating data, ultimately leading to a course of action. Facilitated change presumes commitment on the part of the group to explore alternatives, and investing time and resources to engage in collective activities among the group. The underlying assumption is based on a constructivist view of the world, whereby truth is socially established by a group of individuals, allowing everyone to be open to understanding how other organizational stakeholders see their world.[26] Through interaction among group members, views can be integrated into a shared mental model.

The facilitator plays a key role in helping the group develop a shared mental model. Guiding the process and providing content help to lead toward a common frame of reference. Although facilitators frequently see themselves as process experts and the client as the expert in content, intervention methods and techniques will vary over time – sometimes more process-focused, at other times also content provision. In addition, the interventions can sometimes be very participative and democratic, at other times more directive, yet both process guidance and content framing play their part in determining the outcome.

## Outcome

A number of outcomes follow a facilitated group intervention. The first is the perceived value of the intervention immediately following the event. The second is the existence of shared mental models among the group participating in the intervention and the third is the one most organizations desire, the successful implementation of the agreed-upon course of action. We will look at what impacts the perceived value of a facilitated event and the existence of shared mental models on the assumption that these are proxies for implementation of an agreed-upon course of action.

## Process guidance

In the everyday business setting, managers regularly suppress reflection and discussion in favor of action because the day-to-day pressures of work make it difficult to take anything other than a short-term view. A key role of a facilitator in group interventions is to guide the process by which unlearning, learning, and decisions on alternatives can develop.[27] Although managers understand their own business and the environment in which they operate, they frequently need a facilitated process to help share, re-evaluate, and exploit existing knowledge. Challenging the collective cognition and underlying organizational behavior involves asking questions. Encouraging the members of the group to participate ensures that a broad range of issues and diverse views are heard and discussed, but also requires the facilitator actively to manage the flow of information between members of the group. The more heterogeneous the group is in terms not only of hierarchical representation, but also of gender, education and other characteristics, the more likely it is that views within the group will differ. These differing views are the impetus to change and learning, and provide the basis on which the group, guided by the facilitator, can develop a shared mental model.

The more the facilitator guides the process in such a way that group members perceive that their views are being heard, the more highly they will rate the value of the intervention in which they have participated and the greater the likelihood that the process will have led to an expansion of the group's thinking. We therefore argue that the facilitator's ability to guide group interventions is positively related to two outcomes: the perceived value of the event and the expansion of the group's thinking. The expansion of the group's thinking is an indication that the group has changed its mental models.

> **HYPOTHESIS 1**
> The facilitator's ability to guide the process is positively related to the perceived value of the event.

> **HYPOTHESIS 2**
> The facilitator's ability to guide the process is positively related to the expansion of the group's thinking.

## Framing

A facilitated process among experienced managers who understand their business and environment helps to exploit their knowledge, yet it may not be sufficient to lead to shared mental models. The role of the facilitator in a group facilitated intervention is to assist managers in articulating their views by summarizing an individual's or the group's view on, for example, their competitive position. The facilitator can provide frameworks in which multiple perspectives can be represented. This essentially means that facilitation moves beyond process and enters the sphere of framing through content. By providing feedback to the group, the participants can reflect upon what has been heard by the facilitator. If the different views have been summarized to the extent that the individuals see themselves being represented, a collective understanding can emerge. By providing frameworks and summarizing discussions, the facilitator is implicitly adding content to the discussion, which can broaden the group's understanding of its own issues.

The more the facilitator is able to summarize discussions and provide frameworks that help to integrate different perspectives, the more highly the group will rate the perceived value of the intervention and the more group members will have been able to expand their thinking. We therefore argue that the facilitator's ability to provide content is positively related to two outcomes: the perceived value of the event and the group's expansion of thinking.

> **HYPOTHESIS 3**
> The quality of framing is positively related to the value of the event.

> **HYPOTHESIS 4**
> The quality of framing is positively related to the expansion of the group's thinking.

# Methodology

Respondents to this study consisted of 27 groups from multinational companies that participated in a one-week IMD "Booster" program between 2001 and 2005. During the program, which essentially was run as a facilitated event, groups charged with key company initiatives were supported to increase their ability to execute the initiatives by conducting a thorough analysis of strategic options and developing realistic plans with critical milestones. At the end of the week, each group member was asked to fill out a questionnaire which evaluated the event on a number of dimensions.

In our sample there were 27 groups with an average of 8.6 individuals. They all came from European multinational companies with more than Swiss Franc 100 million turnover. Each group had a change leader who had sent them to the event and was the person to whom they had to deliver the final analysis of what to do within the scope of the strategic change. The event primarily consisted of group facilitation, although some pure content sessions were also provided. Each group had a dedicated facilitator who had worked with the change leader prior to the event and knew about the group's strategic change.

## Measures

The dependent and independent variables were measured using single items with response options ranging from 1 to 5 which were given by the group. The two dependent variables, value of the event and group expansion of thinking, were evaluated using a scale from 1, "poor," to 5, "excellent." The independent variables were also measured on a five-point scale using single items. Quality of framing was an aggregated measure of all content sessions delivered during the events. During these sessions, the facilitators provided frameworks that helped participants re-evaluate their current mental models. The facilitators' ability to guide the process was based on an evaluation of the group's main facilitator. The control variable was the number of members in the group. Table A1.1 shows the descriptive statistics and correlation coefficients of the 27 groups.

Contrary to hypothesis 1, we did not find a significant relationship between the facilitator's ability to guide the process and the perceived value of the event at the $p < .05$ level. Given the same size ($N = 27$), a significance at the $p < .1$ level suggests that process guidance nonetheless plays an important role. In line with hypothesis 3, we found a significant relationship between the facilitator providing frameworks and the perceived value of the event. We also found support for our predication that process guidance is positively related to the expansion of the group's thinking (hypothesis 2). However, we found no support for a significant relationship between framing and expansion of the group's thinking (hypothesis 4). In both models, the control variable was not significant. Results showed that process guidance is more important for expanding the thinking of the group, while providing frameworks is more important in the group's assessment of the value of the event.

TABLE A1.1  Means, standard deviations, and correlations coefficients

| Variable | Mean | s.d. | 1 | 2 | 3 | 4 |
|---|---|---|---|---|---|---|
| 1.  Value of program | 4.31 | .37 | | | | |
| 2.  Expansion of group-thinking | 4.15 | .49 | .53** | | | |
| 3.  Process guidance | 4.01 | .62 | .54** | .86** | | |
| 4.  Framing | 4.02 | .23 | .74** | .50** | .47* | |
| 5.  Group size | 8.59 | 2.400 | −.17 | .00 | −.02 | −.31 |

NOTES: ** Significant at 0.01 level; * Significant at 0.05 level

# Results

Table A1.2 shows two regression models. Model 1 tested hypotheses 1 and 3 while model 2 tested hypotheses 2 and 4.

TABLE A1.2  Results of regression analysis

| Facilitation outcome | | |
|---|---|---|
| **Variables** | **Perceived program value** | **Expansion of group-thinking** |
| | Model 1 | Model 2 |
| Process guidance | .14* | .00** |
| Framing | .00** | .28 |
| Group size | .83 | .62 |
| R-Square | .25 | .26 |
| F-Statistic | 11.06** | 23.89** |

NOTES: * p < .05; ** p > .01

## Discussion

This study was a response to a more thorough investigation of what determines the outcome of group facilitation interventions. Based on these findings, we can argue that the value of group facilitation depends not only on process guidance but also on the provision of frameworks, but that these two factors are important for different types of outcomes. While process guidance is important in expanding the group's thinking and thereby changing mental models, providing frameworks is an important determinant in the perceived value of facilitation. However, the provision of frameworks is not significantly related to the expansion of group-thinking. Based on these findings, one can argue that the perceived value of a event and expansion of group-thinking are two different constructs. Expansion of group-thinking is a prerequisite of shared mental models and thereby a potential mediator to the third outcome: implementation of agreed-upon courses of action. Although the perceived value of interventions reflected in the immediate assessment of what participants valued is one outcome, ultimate success depends on the ability of the group to implement the agreed-upon course of actions. This suggests that expanding the group's thinking, which will develop a shared mental model and then lead to a commitment for action, may in fact be the more important outcome if change is to occur.

One of the explanations for not finding support for a significant relationship between framing and expansion of the group's thinking could lie in the way facilitators use frameworks. When frameworks provide content without a direct link to the problem under discussion, they may have a limited impact on the group's mental model. When, however, the frameworks are used to summarize a discussion, they are more likely to lead to an expansion of the group's thinking and thereby influence their mental model.

Expansion of group-thinking is a prerequisite of shared mental models as it requires a group to adopt another view of reality. According to theories of social constructivism,[28] if we treat something as reality, then this social construction becomes a real objective entity. A reality can be held together by the collective thoughts of a group. This determines what and how we define situations and leads to a course of action with subsequent behavior. For example, individual reactions to the need for customer segmentation in a business may be entirely divergent, yet after an exchange of views, the group may develop a collective view which is the basis of the action that follows. This implies that groups need to articulate predominant views of what is perceived as important and clarify and test their assumptions in order to develop a view of reality to which the individuals aspire and share. Although these challenging predominant views within the context of an organization frequently remain "blocked" or "unchanged," facilitated group interventions can provide the context within which to question the current view of reality against other competing views. This requires not only looking at the assumptions each individual holds about the organization in which they work but also taking an honest look at where these assumptions originate.[29]

Assuming that individuals are the authors of their own reality, then each individual within a group can choose to rewrite their views of reality. This requires them to be willing to re-examine their paradigms and underlying assumptions. The greater the divergence of views of paradigms among a group of people, the greater the efforts needed on the part of the group during the facilitated event. This is because paradigms at the individual level are anchored in interactions and help reduce uncertainty and make life predictable. At the group level collectively shared mental models form the basis of an organizational course of action. When individuals within a group start from different views of a problem, reframing often allows differences to emerge and through guidance lead to a shared view. Group facilitation enables this process to occur.

# APPENDIX 2

## Facilitator assessment questionnaire

## Skilled facilitators are essential for process success

Facilitation skills are essential to working with groups. But what skills do good facilitators need? Empirical research has identified a list of the most important competencies.[30] It is unsurprising:

- Listens actively
- Uses questions skillfully
- Monitors small group dynamics effectively
- Paraphrases short segments of content
- Stimulates group insights and creativity
- Provides feedback and encourages development of process skills
- Remains neutral
- Completes appropriate follow-up activities
- Uses humor effectively
- Uses appropriate technology and visual aids.

But the more difficult question is: how can the competencies of facilitators be assessed? The following questionnaire will help change leaders and facilitators to identify strengths, weaknesses, and development needs.

## The competency framework

This questionnaire is built to reflect the multiple "levels" at which facilitators operate – based on the competency framework summarized in Table A2.1 below.

The competency framework is built around the process stages of facilitation which have varying complexity and therefore different levels of competencies required at each stage by different groups.

Facilitation is a three-stage process – planning, guiding, and post-event follow-up and implementation.

You will recognize these three stages in both the structure of this book and the sequence of tasks that are undertaken in preparing and delivering facilitation events.

Facilitation events vary, however, in their level of complexity and so require different levels of competence from the facilitator.

Temporary groups with a strong task focus often need only limited facilitation inputs – standard methodologies can be appropriate and valued by participants.

At the other end of the scale, complex permanent teams working on problems with multiple impacts across the organization often need highly tailored tools and processes, combined with facilitation, to explore underlying conflicts driven by organizational structure and roles, group dynamics or individual behaviors and motivations.

No questionnaire or assessment tool can ever be comprehensive. This questionnaire has been built from our research and inspired by the writings of many other researchers and the deep experience of ourselves and other practitioners.

For the change leader, this questionnaire can be used to evaluate facilitators they have worked with in the past. A "new" facilitator could also be asked to conduct a self-assessment so that the change leader could see the results.

For the facilitator, self-knowledge of your own competencies, strengths, and gaps is a foundational competence that everyone should possess. Bluntly, if you are not aware of your limitations, you will attempt more than you are currently capable of – with negative consequences for your clients and yourself. We sincerely hope that this tool will help you to focus and clarify your own development needs.

TABLE A2.1 Competency assessment framework

| | Planning events | Guiding group events | Post-event follow-up and implementation |
|---|---|---|---|
| Level 1 | Goal and task focus<br><br>■ Ensuring consistency of change leader and group objectives | Task-focused tools and activities<br><br>■ Strong control of scope | Task achievement feedback and individual accountability<br><br>■ Evaluation of event outcome |
| Level 2 | Process congruence<br><br>■ Agenda and process design based on goal and task | Structure and tools for task and process<br><br>■ Transparency with group re processes, tools and methodology chosen | Feedback of success and learning<br><br>■ Evaluation of quality of group's decisions and behaviors |
| Level 3 | Process design fit to organizational context<br><br>■ Role and responsibility-based group selection | Exploration and challenge of existing roles<br><br>■ Incorporating an understanding of organizational context into group discussion | Organizational development and design input<br><br>■ Feedback of learning for organization |
| Level 4 | Process design reflects political and relationship issues within the organization<br><br>■ Key stakeholders involved in design of solutions | Exploration and challenge of current behaviors and team dynamics<br><br>■ Handling productive conflict | Input to ongoing team development needs and progress<br><br>■ Assessing team development and impact on change |
| Level 5 | Diagnosis of individual participant positions<br><br>■ Emotions, interests, motivations and opinions re task, process and group | Exploration and change of individual positions<br><br>■ Issues of individual behavior | Input to ongoing individual assessment and development<br><br>■ Assessing individual behavior and impact on change |

## How to complete this questionnaire

1. Complete each question box by rating the facilitator you have worked with or yourself on the scale and then calculate the rating for that competency – as shown in this example:

## Level 1: Goal and task focus

To what extent does the facilitator or do you have *experience* of taking responsibility for the following tasks?

| | ① None ③ Some ⑤ Very extensive experience | | | | |
|---|---|---|---|---|---|
| Managing the detailed coordination of the facilitation event? | ① | ② | ③ | ④ | **❺** |
| Planning how to make effective use of the physical space during your facilitation events? | ① | ② | ③ | **❹** | ⑤ |
| Planning time required for activities within the event agenda? | ① | ② | **❸** | ④ | ⑤ |
| Learning to use new problem-solving methodologies? | ① | ② | **❸** | ④ | ⑤ |
| Total scores per column | **0** | **0** | **6** | **4** | **5** |
| Overall Total | | | | | **15** |
| | | | | | **÷ 4** |
| **Level 1: Assessment rating** | | | | | **3.75** |

2. Insert your rating of the specific level and stage into the competency assessment overview (Table A2.2) to create a high-level analysis of strengths and weaknesses. Once you have completed the entire questionnaire, you will have 15 ratings reflecting the facilitator's competencies of planning, guiding, and post-event follow-up and implementation.

For the change leader, this assessment can help make decisions about whether to continue to use a facilitator or how to supplement the facilitator's weaknesses with other forms of support, for example a second facilitator or greater commitment of the change leader's time. For the facilitator, the competency overview can be used to identify a personal development plan for yourself, or identify co-facilitators who can best complement your skill set.

TABLE A2.2 Competency assessment overview

| | Planning events | Guiding group events | Post-event follow-up and implementation |
|---|---|---|---|
| Level 1 | Goal and task focus<br>1  2  3  4  5 | Task-focused tools and activities<br>1  2  3  4  5 | Task achievement feedback<br>1  2  3  4  5 |
| Level 2 | Process and task congruence<br>1  2  3  4  5 | Structure and tools for task and process<br>1  2  3  4  5 | Feedback of success/learning re process<br>1  2  3  4  5 |
| Level 3 | Process design fit to organizational context<br>1  2  3  4  5 | Exploration and challenge of existing roles<br>1  2  3  4  5 | Organizational development input<br>1  2  3  4  5 |
| Level 4 | Process design reflects political and relationship issues<br>1  2  3  4  5 | Exploration and challenge of team dynamics<br>1  2  3  4  5 | Input to ongoing team development<br>1  2  3  4  5 |
| Level 5 | Diagnosis of individual positions<br>1  2  3  4  5 | Exploration and change of individual positions<br>1  2  3  4  5 | Input to ongoing individual development<br>1  2  3  4  5 |

## FACILITATOR ASSESSMENT QUESTIONNAIRE
### Part 1: Event planning

### Level 1: Goal and task focus

To what extent does the facilitator or do you have *experience* of taking responsibility for the following tasks?

① None   ③ Some   ⑤ Very extensive experience

| | | | | | |
|---|---|---|---|---|---|
| Conducting a needs analysis? | ① | ② | ③ | ④ | ⑤ |
| Agreeing event objectives with change leader? | ① | ② | ③ | ④ | ⑤ |
| Coordinating the logistics of delivering events? | ① | ② | ③ | ④ | ⑤ |
| Selecting problem-solving methodologies? | ① | ② | ③ | ④ | ⑤ |
| Total scores per column | ① | ② | ③ | ④ | ⑤ |
| Overall Total | | | | | |
| | | | | | ÷ 4 |

**Level 1: Assessment rating**

### Level 2: Process and task congruence

To what extent does the facilitator or do you have *experience* of taking responsibility for the following tasks?

① None   ③ Some   ⑤ Very extensive experience

| | | | | | |
|---|---|---|---|---|---|
| Developing group problem-solving agendas in line with event objectives? | ① | ② | ③ | ④ | ⑤ |
| Sequencing problem-solving techniques to develop shared mental models? | ① | ② | ③ | ④ | ⑤ |
| Designing agendas to balance inquiry and advocacy, within one event? | ① | ② | ③ | ④ | ⑤ |
| Agreeing facilitation event plans with the change leader? | ① | ② | ③ | ④ | ⑤ |
| Total scores per column | | | | | |
| Overall Total | | | | | |
| | | | | | ÷ 4 |

**Level 2: Assessment rating**

## Level 3: Process design fit to organizational context

To what extent does the facilitator or do you have *experience* of taking responsibility for the following tasks?

① None   ③ Some   ⑤ Very extensive experience

| | | | | | |
|---|---|---|---|---|---|
| Designing facilitation events in cooperation with the change leader? | ① | ② | ③ | ④ | ⑤ |
| Adapting your facilitation process to take account of the organizational context? | ① | ② | ③ | ④ | ⑤ |
| Selecting participants for facilitation events after taking into account the organizational context? | ① | ② | ③ | ④ | ⑤ |
| Selecting participants for facilitation event after understanding the dynamics of the group? | ① | ② | ③ | ④ | ⑤ |
| Total scores per column | | | | | |
| Overall Total | | | | | |
| | | | | | ÷4 |

**Level 3: Assessment rating**

## Level 4: Stakeholder engagement in process design

To what extent does the facilitator or do you have *experience* of taking responsibility for the following tasks?

① None   ③ Some   ⑤ Very extensive experience

| | | | | | |
|---|---|---|---|---|---|
| Engaging with stakeholders to discover their most important priorities? | ① | ② | ③ | ④ | ⑤ |
| Engaging with stakeholders to discover their attitudes toward the priorities of other stakeholders? | ① | ② | ③ | ④ | ⑤ |
| Discovering the sources of power of stakeholders – what they can do to promote or block change? | ① | ② | ③ | ④ | ⑤ |
| Designing facilitation events to ensure adequate debate of stakeholders' most important priorities? | ① | ② | ③ | ④ | ⑤ |
| Total scores per column | | | | | |
| Overall Total | | | | | |
| | | | | | ÷ 4 |

**Level 4: Assessment rating**

## Level 5: Diagnosis of individual participant positions

To what extent does the facilitator or do you have *experience* of taking responsibility for the following tasks?

① None  ③ Some  ⑤ Very extensive experience

| | | | | | |
|---|---|---|---|---|---|
| Designing facilitation events in cooperation with event participants? | ① | ② | ③ | ④ | ⑤ |
| Engaging with individual participants to discover their relationships with key stakeholders? | ① | ② | ③ | ④ | ⑤ |
| Understanding individual participants' motivations to ensure commitment and accountability of results? | ① | ② | ③ | ④ | ⑤ |
| Choosing problem-solving methods that will maximize the contribution of particular individuals to groupwork? | ① | ② | ③ | ④ | ⑤ |
| Total scores per column | | | | | |
| Overall Total | | | | | |
| | | | | | ÷ 4 |

**Level 5: Assessment rating**

# Part 2: Guiding events

## Level 1: Task-focused tools and activities

To what extent does the facilitator or do you have *experience* of the following tasks when working with groups?

① None  ③ Some  ⑤ Very extensive experience

| | | | | | |
|---|---|---|---|---|---|
| Creating clear agreement within the group about the goal of the facilitation event? | ① | ② | ③ | ④ | ⑤ |
| Ensuring participants' points of view are raised and discussed before key decisions are made? | ① | ② | ③ | ④ | ⑤ |
| Ensuring conflict is not negated before key decisions are made? | ① | ② | ③ | ④ | ⑤ |
| Confirming group agreements and decisions? | ① | ② | ③ | ④ | ⑤ |
| Total scores per column | | | | | |
| Overall Total | | | | | |
| | | | | | ÷ 4 |

**Level 1: Assessment rating**

## Level 2: Structure and tools for task and process

To what extent does the facilitator or do you have experience of the following tasks when working with groups?

① None   ③ Some   ⑤ Very extensive experience

| | | | | | |
|---|---|---|---|---|---|
| Establishing group ground rules that are adhered to? | ① | ② | ③ | ④ | ⑤ |
| Explaining to the group the problem-solving processes being used? | ① | ② | ③ | ④ | ⑤ |
| Adapting your facilitation process during events to meet changing group needs? | ① | ② | ③ | ④ | ⑤ |
| Maintaining adequate independence from the group in your role as facilitator? | ① | ② | ③ | ④ | ⑤ |
| Total scores per column | | | | | |
| Overall Total | | | | | |
| | | | | | ÷ 4 |

**Level 2: Assessment rating**

## Level 3: Exploration and challenge of existing roles

To what extent does the facilitator or do you have experience of the following tasks when working with groups?

① None   ③ Some   ⑤ Very extensive

| | | | | | |
|---|---|---|---|---|---|
| Challenging participants to acknowledge the influence of their stakeholder perspective in assessing issues? | ① | ② | ③ | ④ | ⑤ |
| Confronting the use of power by group members to constrain debate of key issues? | ① | ② | ③ | ④ | ⑤ |
| Challenging participants to question the impact of the current organizational context on the feasibility of potential problem solutions? | ① | ② | ③ | ④ | ⑤ |
| Challenging groups to accept responsibility for problem resolution | ① | ② | ③ | ④ | ⑤ |
| Total scores per column | | | | | |
| Overall Total | | | | | |
| | | | | | ÷ 4 |

**Level 3: Assessment rating**

## Level 4: Exploration and challenge of team dynamics

To what extent does the facilitator or do you have *experience* of the following tasks when working with groups?

① None   ③ Some   ⑤ Very extensive

| | | | | | |
|---|---|---|---|---|---|
| Helping individual participants voice their points of view (mental models) so that differences in the group's mental model can be discussed? | ① | ② | ③ | ④ | ⑤ |
| Bringing hidden conflict within the group into the open? | ① | ② | ③ | ④ | ⑤ |
| Helping the group to stay *in* productive conflict *long enough* to ensure an issue is resolved rather than just "parked"? | ① | ② | ③ | ④ | ⑤ |
| Deciding on the amount of guidance necessary given the group's ability to develop a high-quality shared solution? | ① | ② | ③ | ④ | ⑤ |
| Total scores per column | | | | | |
| Overall Total | | | | | |
| | | | | | ÷ 4 |

**Level 4: Assessment rating**

## Level 5: Exploration and change of individual positions

To what extent does the facilitator or do you have *experience* of the following tasks when working with groups?

① None   ③ Some   ⑤ Very extensive

| | | | | | |
|---|---|---|---|---|---|
| Engaging participation and contribution from all members within very diverse groups? | ① | ② | ③ | ④ | ⑤ |
| Creating a climate of safety when participants display initial distrust of the facilitation process? | ① | ② | ③ | ④ | ⑤ |
| Modifying the behavior of difficult participants? | ① | ② | ③ | ④ | ⑤ |
| Building commitment from key participants to solve the issues raised by the facilitation process? | ① | ② | ③ | ④ | ⑤ |
| Total scores per column | | | | | |
| Overall Total | | | | | |
| | | | | | ÷ 4 |

**Level 5: Assessment rating**

## Part 3: Post-event follow-up and implementation

### Level 1: Task achievement feedback

To what extent has the facilitator or have you *completed* the following activities after working with groups?

| | ① Never | ③ Sometimes | ⑤ Always | | |
|---|---|---|---|---|---|
| Provided written summaries of key group decisions following the event? | ① | ② | ③ | ④ | ⑤ |
| Provided summaries of unresolved issues given the objectives? | ① | ② | ③ | ④ | ⑤ |
| Ensured that accountability for the decisions was addressed? | ① | ② | ③ | ④ | ⑤ |
| Debriefed the event objectives with the group? | ① | ② | ③ | ④ | ⑤ |
| Total scores per column | | | | | |
| Overall Total | | | | | |
| | | | | | ÷ 4 |

**Level 1: Self-assessment rating**

### Level 2: Feedback of success and learning regarding process

To what extent has the facilitator or have you *completed* the following activities after working with groups?

| | ① Never | ③ Sometimes | ⑤ Always | | |
|---|---|---|---|---|---|
| Made a (written) evaluation of the effectiveness of the problem-solving methods used with the group? | ① | ② | ③ | ④ | ⑤ |
| Evaluated the group's ability to reach a high-quality shared solution based on the event agenda? | ① | ② | ③ | ④ | ⑤ |
| Evaluated change in the group's behavior? | ① | ② | ③ | ④ | ⑤ |
| Shared your post-event evaluations with the change leader? | ① | ② | ③ | ④ | ⑤ |
| Total scores per column | | | | | |
| Overall Total | | | | | |
| | | | | | ÷ 4 |

**Level 2: Assessment rating**

## Level 3: Organizational development and design input

To what extent has the facilitator or have you *completed* the following activities after working with groups?

| | ① Never | ③ Sometimes | ⑤ Always |
|---|---|---|---|

| | | | | | |
|---|---|---|---|---|---|
| Ensured feedback to key stakeholders (including change leader) of issues within the organization highlighted by the group? | ① | ② | ③ | ④ | ⑤ |
| Provided feedback to the change leader on the ability of the group to create change? | ① | ② | ③ | ④ | ⑤ |
| Evaluated the group's ability to implement organizational change based on the group's commitment to the decisions made? | ① | ② | ③ | ④ | ⑤ |
| Reviewed how far the selection of participants during the planning of events took sufficient account of the organizational stakeholder interests? | ① | ② | ③ | ④ | ⑤ |
| Total scores per column | | | | | |
| Overall Total | | | | | |
| | | | | | ÷ 4 |
| **Level 3: Assessment rating** | | | | | |

## Level 4: Input to ongoing team development

To what extent has the facilitator or have you *completed* the following activities after working with groups?

| | ① Never | ③ Sometimes | ⑤ Always |
|---|---|---|---|

| | | | | | |
|---|---|---|---|---|---|
| Made a (written) evaluation of group effectiveness based on task performance? | ① | ② | ③ | ④ | ⑤ |
| Made a (written) assessment of group development observed during the facilitation process? | ① | ② | ③ | ④ | ⑤ |
| Assessed the group's ability to implement change given their commitment to decisions reached? | ① | ② | ③ | ④ | ⑤ |
| Shared post-event assessments of group development issues with the group and when appropriate with event leader? | ① | ② | ③ | ④ | ⑤ |
| Total scores per column | | | | | |
| Overall Total | | | | | |
| | | | | | ÷ 4 |
| **Level 4: Assessment rating** | | | | | |

## Level 5: Input to ongoing individual development

To what extent has the facilitator or have you *completed* the following activities after working with groups?

| | ① Never | ③ Sometimes | ⑤ Always | | |
|---|---|---|---|---|---|
| Made a (written) evaluation of individual development issues based on behaviors observed within the group? | ① | ② | ③ | ④ | ⑤ |
| Made a (written) assessment of individual learning observed during the facilitation process? | ① | ② | ③ | ④ | ⑤ |
| Assessed individual accountability to group decisions? | ① | ② | ③ | ④ | ⑤ |
| Where appropriate, shared individual assessments with change leader and/or the individuals concerned within an appropriate process? | ① | ② | ③ | ④ | ⑤ |
| Total scores per column | | | | | |
| Overall Total | | | | | |
| | | | | | ÷ 4 |

**Level 5: Assessment rating**

# APPENDIX 3

## Annotated bibliography[31]

Why do theories matter for change leaders and facilitators? Why should they spend their time trying to understand theories? When we used the example in Section 1 which referred to the repair of a washing machine and how you needed to know how it functioned before you could repair it, then you will recognize why understanding more about theories of change and facilitation are important. You need to have a mental model of the causal relationships that set the machine in motion. Such a mental model is based upon theories the technician learned as part of his or her training. Indeed, it is this model that will allow the technician to intervene and hopefully repair the broken machine.

To deal with problems associated with facilitated change, change leaders need to use a blend of practical and personal reasoning and theoretical knowledge. Practical reasoning involves value judgments and taking an ethical stance toward the facilitation engagement and the people who are part of it. It is an ability acquired throughout life as a result of learning from experience, gaining theoretical knowledge, and reflecting upon what one experiences and learns. There is not much we can offer in the context of this book to compensate for lack of personal experience and the ability to judge reasonably. However, theoretical knowledge can be acquired and developed through study and this is what we propose to discuss here. The theoretical knowledge that can help the practice of facilitation is very complex, for the three main reasons given below.

First, facilitation means interacting with human beings. This is notoriously difficult since each human being is a world of his or her own, yet shares the similarities of the human condition. For this reason a sound knowledge of people is needed to develop a fruitful working relationship. Apart from living, observing, and learning from experience, one way to improve this knowledge is through the study of some specific areas that focus on human beings. We are thinking here in general terms of the social sciences and humanities, which have in common the fact that they put human beings and the organizations they create at their core; and in particular we consider some knowledge of psychology as fundamental to an understanding of the nature of facilitation.

Second, the practice of facilitation is based on concepts and interpretations of human beings in interaction. This is an area in which some knowledge of sociology, linguistics, and philosophy – also ethics – can be beneficial. Various writers have shown us how the social world is constructed through the interpretation and constitution of interactions of people.

Third, facilitation processes do not occur in a vacuum; on the contrary, they are embedded in relationships of power. These relationships link all the stakeholders in the process, including the facilitator. In this context, a good knowledge of politics, political philosophy, and political theories can help to disentangle the political web.

We would add that theoretical models and concepts can help because our own actions, intentions, and perceptions are themselves governed by the theories we use to create and recreate the way we conduct our daily lives. The problem is that it is impossible to be fully aware of them. At the moment when we are speaking, acting, and improvising – in other words, living – we are not fully aware of the existence of those models; if we were, we would be unable to act naturally and fluently. Nevertheless, without theories, concepts and models, we would not know where to start, how to conduct the facilitation event, when to intervene or let go, or why we should choose one tactic over another. Theories can give us a better grasp and foresight of the potential effects of our intervention. In other words, without theories, concepts and models we are likely to walk through the dark. Moreover, we would not be making use of the historical path that so many thinkers and practitioners have created before us, to help us conduct our own affairs. Therefore, theories, models, frameworks, and concepts can increase our chances of succeeding and achieving what we set ourselves to achieve. We therefore think it is important to devote time to learning about the foundations of facilitation, as a means toward professional development.

For us, the fundamental starting point is the term "facilitation" – what does it mean? The word "facilitate" originates from the Latin "to make easy." In other words, facilitation helps to improve the internal functioning of a group in order to accomplish its job more easily – whether it be solving a problem, performing a task, making a decision, or a combination of all three.

Discussing group facilitation naturally highlights the group as the key target. Yet a group consists of individuals who are embedded in a larger organizational context. Although the facilitator intervenes within the group, he or she has to have an understanding of the individuals and their motivations as well as the context within which the group operates. The change leader needs to know the theory of how change occurs and what role individuals and groups play in bringing about that change. Figure A3.1

shows the relationship between individuals, the group or team to be facilitated, and the larger organizational context.

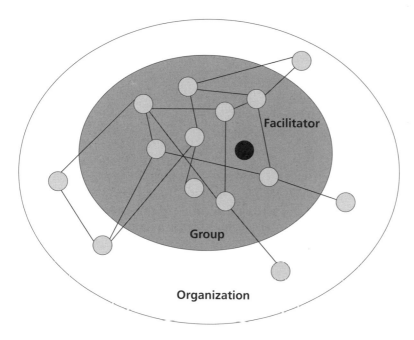

FIGURE A3.1  Role of the facilitator within an organizational web of
relationships

A facilitated event involves intervention at the group level, yet at the
same time the intervention itself has an impact on the organization and the
individuals within the group. In practice, this means that each facilitated
intervention leads to multiple outcomes at different levels. A facilitated intervention is also a process consisting of a sequence of events or activities, and
this can mean a number of processes and actions occurring at different levels.
These can vary in scope from a single person grasping a cognitive train of
thought, an underlying psychological transition in individuals, a series of
decisions taken in a group, up to a reengineering effort at organizational
level in which the group plays a key role. Within this perspective, the focus
is on the sequence of incidents, activities or stages that unfold throughout an
intervention.

Facilitated interventions can be classified into three sequential stages, as
mirrored by the sections in this book:

1. Planning an event – the stage in which the focus is on setting the rules of
   the game, engaging with the organization, the group, and the individuals.

2. Guiding the event – steering discussions among the group and making use of activities that lead to shared mental models.
3. Post-event follow-up and implementation – the stage in which the outcomes are evaluated and implemented within the organization.

When we look at how a facilitation event evolves and the levels of impact that it produces, we can see that it is important for both the change leader and the facilitator to understand the dynamics and underlying processes at each level of impact and at each stage. Figure A3.2 shows that different questions emerge for each level and at every stage. While individuals may be concerned with wanting to improve their personal skills as an outcome, the organizational impact is focused on increasing performance.

Based on the review of the practically oriented literature, we have put together a list of reading material which addresses key questions at each stage and each level of impact. This literature uses a range of theoretical perspectives to explain the role of individuals, groups, and organizations engaged in processes of facilitated change. This list of references is a further resource for any change leader or facilitator wishing to stimulate their thoughts on the underlying theories of facilitation-enabled change.

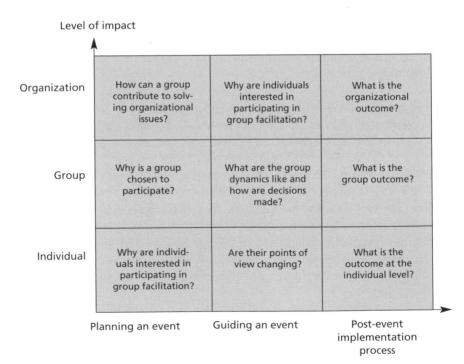

FIGURE A3.2 **Framework of facilitation impact**

Section 1 focuses on the key questions at different stages of a facilitation event at the individual level. Section 2 focuses on key questions across the stages at the group level and Section 3 on the organizational level. For each item, we refer to the key question that the chosen article addresses and provide an executive summary.

## SECTION 1 Individuals, facilitation and change

### What you should know about individuals when planning a facilitated event

Title:     One more time: How do you motivate employees?
Author:    Herzberg, F.
Source:    *Harvard Business Review* **81**(1): 87–96, January 2003

Frederick Herzberg is one of the most important writers on motivation. His work influenced a generation of scholars and managers. He likens motivation to an internal generator and shows that an employee with an internal generator needs no kick in the pants, or as he puts it bluntly, a KITA. For a manager the perennial question is: "How do I get an employee to do what I want?" Herzberg answers that the psychology of motivation is very complex, what has been unraveled with any degree of assurance is small indeed, and the surest way of getting someone to do something is to deliver a KITA. However, not only is it an inelegant solution, but there is also the danger that a manager might get kicked in return. To solve that, he says, companies usually resort to positive KITAs, ranging from fringe benefits to employee counseling. But while a KITA might produce some change in behavior, it doesn't motivate. What really motivates people are intrinsic factors such as achievement, recognition for achievement, the work itself, responsibility, and growth or advancement. The author cites research showing that those intrinsic factors are distinct from extrinsic, or KITA, elements that can lead to job dissatisfaction, such as issues with company administration, supervision, interpersonal relationships, working conditions, salary, status, and job security.

Title:     Towards a process model of individual change in organizations
Authors:   George, J.M. and Jones, G.R.
Source:    *Human Relations* **54**(4): 419–44, April 2001

Using a framework that integrates both the cognitive and affective components of individual sense-making and interpretation, this article analyzes the way the individual change process unfolds when major, second-order changes are required. The authors develop a process model that systematically analyzes the psychology of the individual change process, and, in particular, the sources of resistance to change or inertia. A series of steps in the change process are identified if second-order change is to come about, and a series of testable propositions about the forces that may facilitate or stymie change are developed.

## What you should know about individuals when guiding a facilitated event

Title:      The critical period of disasters: Insights from sense-making and
            psychoanalytic theory
Author:    Stein, M.
Source:    *Human Relations* **57**(10): 1243–61, October 2004

This article could be very helpful to those looking for a deeper understanding of the change process. It focuses on the period during which a disaster unfolds, here called the "critical period." Previous research has shown cases in which sense-making is essential for survival during this period, but it is argued here that there are other cases in which sense-making compounds the problems. Drawing on psychoanalytic theory, it argues that the capacity for anxiety toleration is a moderating variable that influences whether correct sense can be made of the situation. In turn, this tolerance will increase and determine the likelihood of survival.

## What you should know about individual learning to help implement change

Title:      Transferring learning to behavior
Author:    Kirkpatrick, J.
Source:    *Training and Development* **59**(4): 19–20, April 2005

This article focuses on the importance of learning and training programs in the workplace environment. While there are many ways of demonstrating the value of training and facilitation, the best occurs when learning translates into lasting behavioral change. Too often, the subject of learning transfer is lost among the other three levels of evaluation, particularly results measurement. But from a sequential standpoint, it must be done effectively if measures of training value are to be both maximized and meaningful.

## SECTION 2: Groups and how they matter

### What you should know about groups when planning facilitated events

Title:       Virtuoso teams
Authors:   Fischer, B. and Boynton, A.
Source:     *Harvard Business Review* **83**(7): 116–23, July 2005

This article argues that managing a traditional team seems pretty straightforward: gather up whoever's available, give them time and space to do their jobs, and make sure they all play nicely together. However, the authors say, these teams often produce results that are as unremarkable as the teams themselves. When big change and high performance are required, a virtuoso team is far more likely to deliver outstanding and innovative results.

Virtuoso teams, they say, are specially convened for ambitious projects, work with frenetic rhythm, and emanate a discernible energy. Not surprisingly, however, the superstars who make up these teams are renowned for being elitist, temperamental, egocentric, and difficult to work with. As a result, many managers fear that if they force such people to interact on a high-stakes project, the group just might implode.

In this article, the authors put the inner workings of highly successful virtuoso teams on full display through three examples and show how they succeeded by breaking all the conventional rules of collaboration. These range from the way they recruited the best members to the way they enforced their unusual processes, and from the high expectations they held to the exceptional results they produced.

### What you should know about groups while guiding facilitated events

Title:       Decision-making and firm success
Authors:   Ireland, R. and Miller, C.
Source:     *Academy of Management Executive* **18**(4): 8–12, November 2004

The literature on decision-making is reviewed and the authors provide a clear summary of its main points. They focus particularly on issues such as the challenges to decision-making in high-velocity environments, in situations that involve technology and conflict, and in the knowledge and diversity of teams.

## What you should know about groups to ensure implementation

Title:       Thinking about doing: On learning from experience and the flight from thinking

Author:      Levine, D.

Source:      *Human Relations* **55**(10): 1251–68, October 2002

The relationship between learning, thinking, and doing is explored here to great effect. The article describes a case study of a course in group dynamics in which the students wish to learn about groups simply by being in a group. It challenges a given notion of the absolute value of learning from experience, showing that if all we have is an experience, all we can learn is the inevitability of repeating it. This makes learning from experience the enemy of creativity, as its purpose is not to discover what might be, but to assure the reproduction of what is. In this sense, therefore, learning from experience means failing to learn from experience. Failure to learn from experience is linked to fear of thinking. When the group is imagined to be a refuge from thinking, appeal to learning by doing expresses the need to replace learning with belonging. It is a smart and helpful article.

# SECTION 3: Organizational learning and change

## What you need to know about organizational learning that will be the starting point of change

Title:       Sound from silence: On listening in organizational learning

Authors:     Jacobs, C. and Coghlan, D.

Source:      *Human Relations* **58**(1): 115–38, January 2005

At an intersubjective level, one of the central challenges for organizational learning is the development of a shared language, since this is a prerequisite for shared understanding in a community. In this respect, social learning theory suggests communities of practice as loci, and discourse as the medium of such learning. This article shows that rather than knowledge acquisition, social learning refers to identity formation through competent participation in a discursive practice. Listening as a central, yet so far neglected, element of discursive practice involves the constitution of a relational basis that allows for intersubjective meaning generation.

## What you should know about organizational learning that guides change

Title:       Organizational learning: A socio-cognitive framework
Authors:   Akgun, A.E., Lynn, G.S. and Byrne, J.C.
Source:    *Human Relations* **56**(7): 839–68, July 2003

Organizational learning has attracted many researchers and practitioners from different fields and become a popular topic in business and academia. This article examines the subject from the perspective of social cognition and is one of a handful of studies that cross-fertilize social cognition and organizational learning. It argues that social cognition explains the organizational learning process better by integrating fragmented studies on the processes of learning. Therefore the study proposes that organizational learning is an outcome of reciprocal interactions of the processes of information and knowledge acquisition, information and knowledge dissemination, information and knowledge implementation, sense-making, memory, thinking, unlearning, intelligence, improvization, and emotions, which are connected by organizational culture.

## What you should know about decision-making to ensure strategic change

Title:       Stop making plans; start making decisions
Authors:   Mankins, M. and Steele, R.
Source:    *Harvard Business Review* **84**(1): 76–84, January 2006

This article emphasizes the role of decision-making in strategic planning and organizational effectiveness. When strategic planning fails, it is usually because it is an annual process or is focused on individual business units, and conflicts with the way executives make important strategy decisions. The result is that managers make their decisions outside the planning process and without rigorous analysis or debate. To ensure rigorous debate, facilitated events can help to bridge the gap between planning and decision-making. A change in the timing and focus of the strategic planning process or using a decision-making model that spans the entire company produces better results.

## What you need to know about agents of change to ensure implementation

Title:      Your company's secret change agents
Authors:    Pascale, R.T. and Sternin, J.
Source:     *Harvard Business Review* **83**(5): 72–80, May 2005

In this article the authors argue that within every organization there are a few individuals who find unique ways of looking at problems that seem impossible to solve. Although these change agents start out with the same tools and access to resources as their peers, they are able to see solutions where others do not. They find a way to bridge the divide between what is happening and what is possible. These positive deviants are the key, the authors believe, to a better way of creating organizational change. They are the people with whom facilitators need to make sure they connect when trying to bring change into organizations. The authors also create a series of six steps to help implement change in organizations. Throughout the steps, the leader must suspend his or her traditional role in favor of more facilitatory practices.

# APPENDIX 4

# Sample facilitation exercises

## Ideas and examples showing different ways to facilitate group tasks

This section walks you through a few short facilitation exercises so that you – whether as change leader or facilitator – can see how others have applied the principles outlined in this book.

These exercises are selected in the context of facilitating a group which has to make a change in an organization. Our purpose is *not* to provide you with "the best" or "unique" facilitation exercises – there are many good books on these and even a simple internet search will enable you to access many exercises published on the web. But these are exercises that have worked within the context of IMD and for others.

A number of the exercises are included in our example agenda in Section 2. Reviewing the exercises and agenda together will help you to see how they support different elements of an agenda's "red thread" and help groups to move from issue investigation to decisions and then action planning.

Instructions and suggested facilitator interventions are provided for each exercise. You can therefore see how these exercises will lead to more inquiry or advocacy to help develop a shared mental model.

The sample exercises[32] included here are given in the table below.

| Exercise and focus | Description and purpose |
| --- | --- |
| Fortune Success<br>Focus: *Advocacy* | Creating a shared ambition for the group and so a shared understanding of its task |
| Business Lifeline<br>Focus: *Inquiry* | Reflection on past experiences to explore the underlying strengths and weaknesses of the organization |

| Exercise and focus | Description and purpose |
|---|---|
| Hopes and Fears<br>Focus: *Inquiry* | Sharing their hopes and fears about the task, groups identify the critical tasks and key risks to be managed in order to achieve their vision or ambition |
| Project Elevator Pitch<br>Focus: *Advocacy* | Defining the project objective, strategic fit, and measures of success in 100 words. This clear, shared understanding of the group's task and objectives increases its effectiveness |
| Hall of Fame and Hall of Shame<br>Focus: *Inquiry* | Learning from previous change implementations and about the barriers to change in the organization |
| Beat Yourself<br><br>PART 1: Understanding competitors<br>Focus: *Inquiry* | Understanding what competitors are doing to add value, their market positioning and their strategies |
| PART 2: Competitive attacks<br>Focus: *Advocacy* | Stress testing group solutions by finding out what in the group solution is unique and different and creates real competitive advantage or innovation – and what does not |
| New Behaviors and Capabilities<br>Focus: *Advocacy* | Defining priorities, tasks, and changes required to support implementation of their problem solution |
| Decision Process and Decision Power<br>Focus: *Action planning* | Tactical planning of how to consult stakeholders and win approval of the change agenda |
| Challenging Perspectives<br>Focus: *Action planning* | Planning how to manage the potential reactions of key stakeholders |
| How are we doing as a team?<br>Focus: *Inquiry* | Structured questions provide the group with a process to review how it works together and becomes more effective and focused |

## Fortune Success

Fortune Success is, as you will see, a visioning exercise. Its purpose is to create a shared ambition for a group. (In discussing this, we will use the phrase "shared ambition," simply because there is so much debate about what is and is not a "vision.") Put yourself three years in the future. You are being interviewed by *Fortune* magazine to explain your dramatic achievement in transforming your company to become recognized as the most successful in the world. Here some questions that the group could focus on:

- How do you define global leadership for your company?
- What are the key indicators of your success?
- What were the major challenges you faced along the way?

To help a group be effective and efficient, the shared ambition must be clear, specific, and commonly understood. As such, this exercise promotes *advocacy* – seeking to define a starting point and shared ambition that are relevant to the group and the organizational context.

To facilitate a group toward that objective, you the facilitator need to have in your own mind a clear understanding of two things:

- What is a shared ambition – what criteria must be satisfied for this to be achieved, and how you will know when the group has truly built a shared goal?
- What process must the group go through to build a shared ambition – and so what interventions and process guidance must you give the group?

*What is a shared ambition?* The simple answer to this is an objective which the group has agreed to pursue. But while this is true, it is an incomplete answer. A good shared ambition has the following characteristics. It is:

- *Clear* – both the objective and the planned process of achieving that objective must be defined in simple, vivid terms, using words which are not open to misinterpretation.
- *Specific* – the objective and planned process must be detailed enough to prevent misinterpretation and confusion in the group. It will also enable ongoing assessment of progress toward, and feasibility of, the objective and planned process to be made. Finally, it ensures that changes to the objective and overall process will be explicit and noticed.
- *Commonly understood* – what is "clear and specific" for one individual can often be unclear and vague for another – or clear and specific but with a different interpretation. For a shared ambition to be commonly understood, the group must go through a process of building and *testing* a shared language – finding commonly understood terms in which to talk and test and explore their assumptions to ensure that their common language is truly understood.

If the objective is vague and the planned process of getting there is not clearly defined, then three problems will slow the group down:

- Different individuals will have different understandings of the group's objective. This will create ongoing conflict about what they are trying to achieve. It will also make the group inefficient, for example inconsistent priorities between individuals will slow down the decision processes.
- Individual behavior in the group will be guided by different objectives, values, beliefs, and priorities. This leads to inconsistency, incoherence of actions, and decisions by individuals and subgroups within the group. This in turn increases confusion within the group because its members will not agree on what individual contributions are valuable in moving toward that goal.
- The group will be unable to concisely explain to other stakeholders what it wants to achieve and why. This will limit its ability to enrol stakeholder support and access the resources it needs.

*What process must the group go through to build a shared ambition?* To build a shared ambition a group must go through a basic cycle of creating options, evaluating options, selecting, prototyping, and then refining its goals. As such, your role as facilitator is to help the group go through those phases as efficiently as possible. This does not only mean time efficiency, although that is always a key constraint. Maximizing the creativity of the group, and the communication and effectiveness of their decision processes, is also key.

## Business Lifeline

Business Lifeline is an exercise to create reflection and learning from past organizational experiences. Initially, the exercise involves individual reflection and then, as a team, drawing a business history for the past two years.

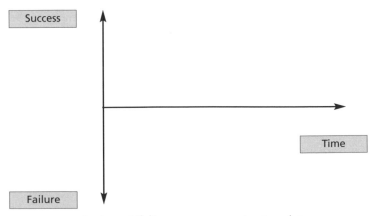

FIGURE A4.1  Business Lifeline – group exercise template

Individually, and then as a team, draw your view on how you have done managing this business. Write short notes about the high points and low points, major "prouds" and "sorrys," accomplishments and failures, and transition points.

The purpose is to explore the underlying strengths and weaknesses of the organization. As such, it promotes deeper *inquiry* into the organizational context of the group's task. By looking back on the past successes and failures of their business, the group can extract what contributed to the highs and lows, why they succeeded and failed, what the *real* reasons were behind the success and failure.

To facilitate a group toward this objective, the facilitator needs to focus on:

■ Ensuring that collective myths and urban legends are challenged – that *new* reflection occurs and *honest* opinions are voiced.
■ Helping the group to question and acknowledge how much internal versus external events and circumstances contributed to successes and failures.

*Ensuring that collective myths and urban legends are challenged* is necessary to ensure that new learnings are created. Research shows that left alone, groups will spend two-thirds of their time talking about what they all know already, and only one-third actually listening to information that only some group members know. Typically, when given this exercise, groups will tend to rehearse and repeat the stories and explanations of past performance that have been shared many times before. Left alone, they will spend a lot of time repeating those stories and never, or only after a long preamble, discuss other explanations.

Your role as a facilitator is to *challenge* those collective myths and so to *speed up* the progress of the group to the stage of questioning and re-examination of the real causes of past performance.

*Helping the group question and acknowledge how much internal versus external events and circumstances contributed to past successes and failures* is necessary to ensure that the group reaches more *objective* answers.

Individuals and groups commonly fall into what psychologists refer to as the "fundamental attribution error" summarized below:

■ We see our own successes as more influenced by our own actions than is true.
■ We assign too much weight to external events in explaining our failures.
■ Conversely, in explaining the successes of others, we assign too much weight to external events.
■ In explaining the failures of others, we see them as more influenced by their own actions than is true.

By asking questions about the truth and reality of explanations of past successes and failures, the facilitator can play a big role in helping the group to escape from these natural but unhelpful fallacies. It also helps to create a sense of urgency among the group – a key first step in any change process.

## Hopes and Fears

Sharing their hopes and fears about the task, groups identify the critical tasks and the key risks to be managed in order to achieve their vision or ambition. Individually, groups are asked to take a few minutes and write down:

■ *Your greatest fears for this group and its task.* What would be the worst outcome? What might go wrong? What could cause the group to fail?
■ *Your greatest hopes for this group and its task.* What would be the best outcome? What would it be great to achieve? What could cause the group to excel? What would be a visible signal of real success?

Then as a group, or in subgroups they share their hopes and fears and discuss them.

The purpose of this exercise is to prompt this discussion and disclosure within the group. By managing when and how the group reveals its hopes and fears, facilitators can ensure that those hopes and fears are captured and the group consciously works to address them. Groups build a common understanding of their goals and potential problems.

Hopes and Fears is an exercise to create disclosure. Often that disclosure is of emotions which may or may not be rational. And it is an exercise that the group needs to do sooner rather than later in its work together.

If the disclosure of hopes and fears is not managed, it will happen in small subgroups, in private, or not at all. And then the group as a whole will work in denial. Fears and risks will not be discussed. The group's risk of producing a solution that cannot be implemented will increase.

## Project Elevator Pitch

To be effective in working together, a group must build its own shared expectations of what it aims to achieve, why, how, and with what resources. The group must decide:

■ *Outputs:* what it considers to be a feasible objective, how it sees the context of that objective (including which stakeholder needs are most important and why), and what the group thinks "success" will look like for this task

■ *Inputs:* whether the resources available to it are adequate.

The sooner this happens, the more quickly the group will become effective in tackling the task in hand. As such, building a shared interpretation of its objectives for the group to start from is a key task of every facilitator.

The group should attempt this task, however, *after* having confirmed its understanding of the expectations of other stakeholders.

Defining a "project elevator pitch" (a short statement of the group's objective and the rationale underpinning it) can be a useful tool to help a group start (and finish) this conversation.

---

**Defining objectives and expectations – creating an elevator pitch**

The "elevator pitch" concept is commonly used within the world of venture capital. The idea is that you, an entrepreneur, find yourself in an elevator with a venture capitalist. This is your one chance to sell your business idea to this potential investor – and so in only 60 seconds you must define the purpose, key messages, and value of your idea, using 100 words or less.

---

The process of creating an elevator pitch is often a powerful way to develop a shared understanding within groups of their task and objectives. By defining in a few words the key objective, measures of success, strategic relevance, and most significant challenges in their project, groups create some shared language about their task and some initial agreement about their priorities.

## Hall of Fame and Hall of Shame

Hall of Fame and Hall of Shame is often an exercise to use after the first steps of the change program have been taken. It can be used as an "after-action review" exercise to debrief with the team and create reflection and learning from its first experiences of implementing the change; to explore the underlying strengths and weaknesses of the organization and change program; and to adapt and develop implementation plans as necessary. In this form, the exercise promotes inquiry – focused on reflection and learning.

## Hall of Fame and Hall of Shame – drivers of and barriers to progress

Do you have a strategic transformation agenda? In the project areas where you are making (or not) significant progress, what are the drivers (or barriers) of the progress? You have 10 points in total to assign across the five categories below (that is, the total of all points is 10).

☐ Clear vision
☐ Clear agenda
☐ Clear roles and empowerment
☐ Strong project leadership or ownership
☐ Access to resources

With adaptation, the exercise can also be used to look *forward*. Groups can be asked to create a future Hall of Fame – a vision or shared ambition as demonstrated in the Fortune Success exercise. Equally, they can create a future Hall of Shame – the worst imaginable future. Using these exercises to look into the future can bring out the hopes and fears of the group and identify the critical tasks and the key risks to be managed in order to achieve its vision or ambition. In this forward-looking form, the exercise promotes *advocacy* – bringing the group to state what it wants to achieve and what it wants to avoid.

To facilitate a group toward these objectives, the facilitator needs to have a clear understanding of:

- What a shared ambition is – as discussed in the Fortune Success exercise instructions.
- The process they must guide the group through to build a shared ambition.
- How to ensure that collective myths and legends are challenged – as discussed in the Business Lifeline exercise instructions.
- How to help the group question and acknowledge the risk of fundamental attribution error (as explained in the Business Lifeline exercise) to ensure it more objectively identifies the causes of past successes and failures.

## Beat Yourself – instructions

This is an exercise designed to help the group develop or reinforce a sense of urgency for change. Current strategies and plans may no longer be sufficient to remain competitive. By putting groups in the role of the competition, they are likely to understand the need for change – the starting point for any process of change. It can also serve to make the plans developed more robust against competitive attacks.

By putting groups in the role of the competition, it helps them to find out what is unique and different about their strategies and where they do not create real competitive advantage or innovation. For the purposes of this exercise, groups are asked to take the role of senior management of Competitor X (insert company name). The challenge is to develop a plan of attack in response to the strategy.

The important elements in this exercise are to:

■ Encourage the group to "walk a mile in another man's shoes."
  – It can be the first group exercise – particularly if internal knowledge of the value proposition, market positioning, and current strategies of competitors are less understood.
  – It can also serve to test existing plans against potential competitive responses and thereby becomes one of the later exercises.
  – This can be done by investigating multiple competitors. Breaking into subgroups will produce more diverse analysis of the strategies. Smaller subgroups are also more comfortable for voicing perceived weaknesses.

*Option 1: Understanding competitors* – helps to evaluate current strengths against the competition and so focuses on inquiry:

■ Ensure the group explores different competitors to fully understand their value propositions, market positioning and strategies.
  – This ensures testing internal assumptions about competitor's strengths against the existing organizational set-up.

*Option 2: Responding to competitive attacks* – helps to ensure robustness of strategic plans and thereby focuses on advocacy:

■ Ensure the group debates and considers the possible responses of competitors properly.
  – Superficial responses to competitor challenges will be tempting. Often the group will be impatient to "finish" by this point in the facilitation process.
  – Specific challenges or weaknesses may be denied. Often the group – or particular group members – will have a strong attachment to particular elements of the strategy or solution. This can be because of their particular interests as a stakeholder ("investing in CRM will make life better for my team") or their attachment to an idea they have worked hard to create ("we fought for four hours about how to attract that customer group, don't tell us we'll never win them from the competition").

## New Behaviors and Capabilities

The purpose of New Behaviors and Capabilities is to turn the group's shared ambitions and learning into tangible conclusions about priorities, tasks, and required changes.

**To achieve our potential and ambitions we must**

| Keep | Develop | Stop doing |
|------|---------|------------|
| 1. | 1. | 1. |
| 2. | 2. | 2. |
| 3. | 3. | 3. |
| 4. | 4. | 4. |
| 5. | 5. | 5. |
| 6. | 6. | 6. |
| 7. | 7. | 7. |
| 8. | 8. | 8. |

The exercise is used for "framing" what has previously happened in the organization and then translating that understanding into solutions and action plans through *advocacy* and *productive conflict*. Conflict during this exercise is inevitable and essential. It is part of building commitment to decisions and implementation.

The exercise is designed to shift the group to look *forward*. To facilitate a group toward these objectives, the group must have already:

■ Developed a shared ambition.
■ Explored the strengths and weaknesses of the organization, the change program, and any existing implementation plans.

In addition, to use this exercise successfully, a facilitator needs to have a clear understanding of a shared ambition and barriers to executing this ambition before moving to new behaviors and capabilities.

## Challenging Perspectives

Challenging Perspectives is an exercise to use to break out of groupthink and ensure that the group actively considers the potential views and reactions of other stakeholders. As such, *inquiry* is the focus. The exercise challenges groups to think widely about the organization and who needs to be consulted and why for the change implementation to be successful.

The exercise has three stages:

- Identifying who are the stakeholders.
- Identifying the needs, priorities, and fears of each stakeholder group.
- Planning how to engage and communicate with each stakeholder group.

Challenging Perspectives is an exercise to help groups avoid coming to conclusions unacceptable to other stakeholders. Group members are asked to let go of their subjectivity and self-interest.

The facilitator's key role in this exercise is to challenge the assumptions and stereotypes which group members bring regarding each stakeholder group. Good searching and innocent questions can force the group to reflect on the needs, priorities, and fears of each stakeholder group.

## Decision Process and Decision Power

Decision Process and Decision Power is an exercise to help the group do tactical planning as to which stakeholders must be consulted to validate, modify, improve, and approve the change agenda. In doing so, it focuses groups on implementation – feasibility questions, stakeholder communication, resources, and political support. The underlying question is: What is required to turn the group's shared solutions and shared mental models into action and change?

*Task 1: Identify the real decision processes inside the organization*
- Who really makes the decisions?
- How much power and freedom to choose does each decision-maker really have?
- On whom do the most powerful decision-makers rely for advice?
- What is the sequence of decisions?

Importantly, who is outside any "official" decision-making process but can block or accelerate decisions, change and/or access to resources?

Map the key decision-makers and influencers on Figure A4.2 in the sequence in which they will "touch" your project. Each box represents a decision-maker and the strength of their support or opposition. Inside each box, identify the key people who will influence them and the most important issues which concern them.

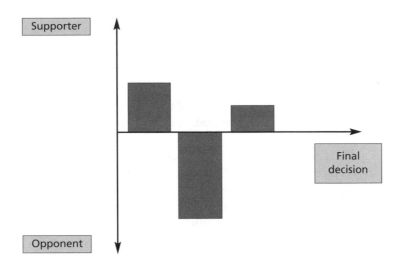

FIGURE A4.2 **Stakeholder assessment map**

*Task 2: Create specific "mobilization plans" for each decision-maker and influencer*
Create clear, powerful, detailed arguments that will influence stakeholders to support change. Plan how, when, and who you will use to deliver these messages.

This exercise is important because it promotes *inquiry* and, if successful, shifts the group's mindset in a way that can significantly improve the probability of implementation success. Having gone through the pain and conflict of building their proposed solution, at this point in the facilitation process groups are often firmly in the mindset of advocacy – proposing and persuading. This exercise shifts them back into greater openness to listen to other opinions.

To facilitate a group toward this objective, the facilitator needs to focus on ensuring that:

- All key stakeholders have been identified.
- The priorities, interests, and needs of each group of stakeholders have been identified.
- The different stakeholders have been prioritized, for example by using the mapping tool in the Challenging Perspectives exercise.

## How Are We Doing as a Group?

This is an exercise designed to help the group improve its effectiveness in working together. Actively reflecting on this question helps the group to focus on process separately from task. It can be viewed as a maintenance activity – but an essential one. By reviewing group effectiveness proactively, the group reduces its risk of descending into destructive conflict and raises its productivity, using its time more effectively.

Structured questions provide the group with a process to make the review of its work more effective and focused.

For this exercise to be productive, the facilitator must ensure that the discussion does not descend into a simple conversation. Focus on:

- *Working through the questions and topics raised.* The worksheet questions provide coverage of many potential issues. If only some are discussed, the group may miss or avoid discussing important barriers to its productivity.
- *Summarizing and closing topics.* Ensure all issues are discussed – but not endlessly.
- *Depersonalizing conflict.* Some causes of group ineffectiveness will be personal and relate to how an individual works with others. However, focus discussion on *specific* examples and the *effect* of behavior. This can then be used to establish and reinforce *general* ground rules for the group.
  - For example "John never turns his mobile phone off and it bugs me" is too general, and a response of "John must turn his phone off" is too specific.
  - "Yesterday John left his mobile phone on, and at 9.30 he answered it and left the room for 15 minutes. When he came back, the group had to stop work to bring him back up to speed. Its unproductive" is more specific. Similarly, a conclusion of "We won't allow interruptions when the group is all together" is more useful.

Individually, groups are asked to complete the attached group effectiveness appraisal, rating their group's performance on each item on a scale of 1 to 5 (1 = very poor; 5 = excellent); then as a group they are asked to discuss the scores seen for each item.

They are to focus most time and inquiry on items where scores are very high, very low or vary widely.

Then they should ensure they agree and document specific changes that they will make.

TABLE A4.1 Example group effectiveness appraisal sheet

| | Your rating for the group | Other group member scores 1 = poor, 5 = great | | | | | | | | | Your notes |
|---|---|---|---|---|---|---|---|---|---|---|---|
| The group has a clearly agreed objective | | | | | | | | | | | |
| The group respects the ground rules | | | | | | | | | | | |
| Communication is sufficient – all group members know enough to be able to make their full contribution | | | | | | | | | | | |

# APPENDIX 5

## Practical issues – location, equipment and logistics

The management of practical issues – locations, equipment and logistics – is an essential element in the successful design of a facilitation event. Often dismissed lightly, often "delegated" with little guidance or follow-up, location, equipment and logistics and are vital things to get right. If forgotten or mishandled, they will undermine the group's commitment to the process, and/or the facilitator or change leader's relationship with the group.

## Location

Selecting a suitable venue is critical to the success of the event. The location sends a message about how much you value and respect the group and its potential contribution. Ultimately, you must put yourself in the position of a participant attending the event and ask whether the venue inspires or stifles you.

Questions to ask about any proposed venue:

■ Is the location readily accessible to everyone who may attend, or have I just chosen somewhere that is convenient for or familiar to me?
■ Are the lighting, heating, and air conditioning adequate?
■ Is the available space versatile or are there large fixed features that would make it difficult or impossible to have flexible seating arrangements?
■ Are there any restrictions, for example sticking posters on walls, noise, and so on?

## Arranging the room

Having selected a suitable venue, you need to create an optimal learning environment. You will often want to rearrange the layout during the event, so select a venue that is flexible.

Plan your room use and confirm you can use the room as you plan. Recently, for example, two days before running a Deep Dive rapid prototyping exercise[33] for 95 people, we learned that participants would not be allowed to stick flip-chart paper to the walls of the hotel conference hall.

Whatever room layout you choose, some general rules apply:

- Make sure that all participants can see the facilitator.
- Provide for break-out areas in the room (or in close proximity) for subgroup working.
- Consider whether sitting at tables will be beneficial or actually detrimental to the learning experience. Sometimes groups need desk space to work together, and sometimes not, for example standing up to work together on flip charts can re-energize a tired group.
- Avoid positioning people so that they can see out of the windows.
- Try to have a separate area for meals and refreshments.

A selection of common room layouts is given in Figure A5.1, together with their relative benefits and limitations.

## Equipment

Most facilitators have a small repertoire of technology and equipment. A projector, a laptop, some overhead transparencies, some wall posters, some games for icebreakers and introductions in the group, sometimes a DVD player.

Usually, facilitators, change leaders, and guest speakers with groups use material they are familiar with – and familiarity breeds contempt. Taking the time to confirm availability of equipment, testing it both before arriving at the venue and on site, and ensuring you have substitute equipment or fallback plans are all, however, essential.

Wasting the group's time is a cardinal sin and quickly demotivates them. Making them wait while you fix technical problems is not just embarrassing, it directly affects the quality of their output.

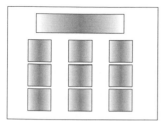

### Classroom setting

This configuration puts the facilitator firmly in control and encourages participants to pay attention. It is suited to plenary activities such as going through the agenda and concluding the event. Consider also angling the tables to encourage more group interaction.

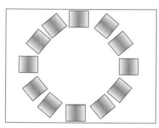

### Half-moon

This arrangement also promotes a focus on the centre, but it allows for more group interaction. This is a good alternative for plenary events when you wish to encourage a discussion among a group of participants.

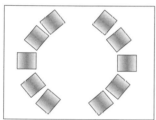

### Circular

This set-up promotes group focus and equality and encourages discussion. It is a standard config-uration for groupwork.

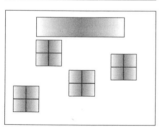

### Open clam

Splitting the circle into two to form an "open clam" is a useful alternative; it can be less intim-idating and also allows greater freedom of movement.

### Cluster groups

This arrangement creates a focus on small groups and focuses less on the facilitator and the group as a whole. It is most useful when you wish to alternate between plenary events and groupwork with a minimum of disruption.

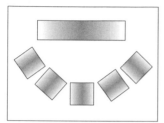

### Boardroom

"Boardroom" and "racecourse" layouts are not recommended for facilitative learning or, indeed, any other sort of training. The many drawbacks include:

- It is difficult for the facilitator to effectively maintain eye contact with extended rows of participants.
- It is impossible for participants to converse in anything larger than pairs.
- It instantly creates a hierarchical environment.

FIGURE A5.1 **Room layouts**

## Managing the logistics of large groups

Large events (30+ people) can be extremely effective and can actually be easier to manage than smaller events as the sheer numbers of people create energy and momentum. Consider, however, which specific aspects of the overall program actually benefit from such a large group. For example, a large group can be very effective in identifying lots of process problems but will be less efficient in designing the solutions.

Large group events require very careful design. The following guidelines will help:

- Be realistic (with both yourself and the participants) about what can be achieved in the time available.
- Be flexible – have tasks and materials prepared but be ready to improvise.
- Accept that some people will arrive late so start with some non-essential activities.
- Be prepared to dictate the ground rules at the start of the event. Pay particular attention to meeting people's expectations from the event and the finish time.
- Keep people alert – maximize activity. Alternate plenary and small group activities.
- Actively manage questions and answers or the whole event can be disrupted by the sheer volume of questions. Solutions include:
  - postponing all questions to designated Q&A events
  - organizing participants into groups and taking only one or two questions from each group.
- Dispense with a formal registration process at the start as this can easily cause an unacceptable bottleneck. Ensure, however, that someone records names and contact details of participants and that this information is complete before the event finishes.
- Maximize the available space – if necessary, coats, bags, and so on can be stored separately and tables and chairs dispensed with to make room for activities.
- Maximize the use of wall posters instead of slides – people can review them at their leisure, they divert people's attention around the room, and encourage movement.
- Be realistic about breaks (and less flexible about unscheduled breaks and restart times).

## Managing subgroups within events

During the event, you will want to organize the participants into a variety of different-sized subgroups for a number of activities. Examples of likely configurations include:

- Pairs for short (one minute) discussions, for example "What are the top three causes of time being wasted in the company?"
- Groups of three or four for longer exploration of ideas and issues, for example "Why is there an apparent lack of customer focus in the company?"
- Pairs or groups of three for sharing and discussing personal reflections, for example "Discuss a situation where each of you felt you were treated disrespectfully."
- Groups of four or five for other work such as brainstorming, for example "How could we improve customer intimacy in the company?"
- Groups of the appropriate size for role plays, games, and simulations.
- Larger groups if you wish to spread specialist knowledge held by only a few participants, for example if you are discussing a manufacturing issue, you should have at least one person with some production experience in each group.

In deciding on the ideal group size for a particular activity, you must weigh the benefits of having more people (diversity of ideas, and so on.) against the greater time taken for larger groups to gel and the risk of individuals becoming disengaged or marginalized. The appropriate size will depend on the nature of the participants and the dynamics of the event as well as the activity itself.

## Forming subgroups

Forming subgroups is an activity in itself; thoughtful use of a variety of techniques will ensure the desired group characteristics, enliven the event, and minimize the time wasted.

- *Random groups:* These are good as mixers early on in events; forming them is quick, simple and fun. There are many ways to form groups randomly including:
  - Numbering off – decide how many groups you want and then participants can number off, for example 1, 2, 3, 4, 1, 2 ...
  - Jigsaw – cut up a number of pictures (one for each group) and hand

out the pieces; participants form themselves into groups by putting
together the jigsaw.

- Farmyard – choose an animal for each group, and hand out slips of
  paper with the different animal names written on them; participants
  then have to form themselves into groups by miming or imitating
  their animal noise.

- *Structured groups:* These can ensure that there is a good mix of back-
  grounds, disciplines, and so on in order to provide a range of viewpoints
  in each group. Often it is easiest to gather people together into similar
  groups first (for example technical, administrative, sales staff, men,
  women, and so on) in order to divide them up into suitably diverse
  groups.

- *Preset groups:* If the precise composition of groups is critical or you want
  to use the same groups over an extended period of time, it is best to
  plan them in advance and simply announce or display the results to
  participants.

- *Self-selecting:* One way of breaking a larger issue down into its component parts is for each group to examine/discuss a specific sub-issue. In
  this situation, it is often best to allow people to choose the group whose
  task best suits their interest and/or expertise. Tasks can be allocated or
  participants can suggest topics and then form groups around them.

*Note* that when allowed freedom to self-select their subgroups, participants will often form themselves into larger groups than required. If you
specify groups of four, be prepared for some groups of five or six. In effect,
participants often "vote with their feet" when forming their own subgroups.
This can signal some important information, for example that one of the
subgroups has a task that many participants see as more important, challenging or high-profile than other tasks on offer. When there has been conflict in
the group, it can also signal loyalties – who sides with whom.

# APPENDIX 6

# Checklists

## Memory joggers for good design, guidance and follow-up/implementation of facilitation events

In the following pages you will find a set of checklists which summarize some of the important issues covered in this book. They are a practical tool to help you, the change leader, to ensure that you maximize the effectiveness of facilitation events that you use to create momentum for change. As a change leader, you will also find that working through these checklists with facilitators gives more structure and clarity to your working relationship and mutual expectations.

The checklists cover:

- Planning a facilitated session – the strategic context.
- Selecting a facilitator.
- Establishing the facilitator and change leader relationship.
- Understanding the organizational context – needs analysis.
- Understanding the group structure.
- Event and agenda design.
- Guiding the facilitation event.
- Closing the facilitation event.
- Post-event follow-up.
- Implementation of event outcomes.

## Planning a facilitated session – the strategic context

■ How urgent and important is this change initiative for the organization?
■ What is your initial assessment of the readiness of the organization to accept change and to accept a solution developed by a facilitated group event?
■ Has the overall purpose and strategy of your change initiative been adequately and clearly communicated to all involved in the initiative?
■ Have the objectives, roles, and usefulness of facilitation events within your wider change initiative been agreed with key stakeholders?

## Selecting a facilitator

■ Is your choice of facilitator based on his or her capability to deliver lasting momentum for change for the organization?
■ How will you assess the adequacy of the facilitator's knowledge of the subject area? Skills and experience in managing conflict? Competency to design and guide a facilitation event appropriate to the complexity of the group task? (See Facilitator competency assessment in Appendix 2.)
■ Is an internal or external facilitator more appropriate? Which is important in the context: organizational objectivity/independence or knowledge of the organization and its people?

## Establishing the facilitator and change leader relationship

■ Have the roles, responsibilities, and relationship of the change leader and the facilitator been clearly defined, including responsibilities for key tasks, fees, and resources?
■ Are there clear shared expectations of the change leader's role within the group?
■ Is the facilitator neutral about outcomes – but not neutral about process? Is his or her role and purpose to help the group to develop solutions effectively?
■ Do you, the change leader, and the facilitator both accept that the purpose of facilitation is to seek the best achievable solutions to issues?

## Understanding the organizational context – needs analysis

■ What is required for an adequate needs analysis to be completed? How far will it consider the views and needs of the change leader, participants, and other stakeholders?

■ Has the needs analysis increased your insights into what problems or issues need to be resolved?

■ Do you have an understanding of what would constitute acceptable outcomes to the key stakeholders?

■ Have you obtained all relevant information for the group to work with?

■ Based on the needs analysis, is facilitation the right tool for achieving the desired outcome?

■ Is the change leader truly open to solutions the group may develop? Is the contribution of the group required and valued?

## Understanding the group structure

■ Is this group sufficiently open to change, representative of stakeholders, and knowledgeable to achieve a successful outcome?

■ How does the group currently interact and work together? What are the goals, task, roles, membership, norms, and leadership of the group?
  - Is this group an existing team or a new group of individuals working together?
  - Has the group or organization experienced significant change recently?

■ Are learning objectives a part of the facilitation event?

## Event and agenda design

■ What is the purpose of the facilitation event? How does it fit in with other elements of organizational changes?

■ Is there a clear "red thread" in the agenda – a sequence of relevant tasks and activities using *framing*, new information and analysis tools, and *conflict engagement* to guide the group through *inquiry* and *advocacy* to develop new understandings of issues, hear opinions, make decisions and, in doing so, develop new shared mental models?

■ Does the agenda present balanced information and analysis tools which will not unduly favor the interests or existing opinions of particular stakeholders?

■ Have you balanced different types of activities and inputs to maintain group energy?

■ Have you planned and allocated responsibility for practical issues such as logistics, location, and equipment?

■ Have you included event breaks and reflection time – formal and informal – to enable participants to digest what they have just discovered, decided or agreed to before moving on?

■ Have you planned how to close the session and ensured that you will have enough time to close it well?

■ Have you included interim change leader briefings in the event design to enable the group to validate and update the change leader with its key decisions and new insights (if the change leader does not participate in the event)?

■ What meetings to review the draft agenda and event design will take place with the change leader, participants, and other stakeholders to build understanding and shared ownership of the facilitation event?

■ What other pre-event communication is required to prepare participants and other stakeholders for the event and to clarify their expectations of what will happen and how they will be communicated with *after* the event?

## Guiding the facilitation event

■ At the start of the event, what will you do to clarify for the group its objectives and expectations about its task, outputs, and the resources available to the group?

　－ When will you communicate the event agenda – how the group will work on its task? In how much detail? How much flexibility is there to adapt the agenda during the event?

　－ How will the facilitator and group establish ground rules – principles, behaviors, and norms to maintain group effectiveness?

　－ What will the facilitator do to establish his or her role within the group as a process expert – helping the group to work together more effectively?

■ *Framing:* Is the facilitator using new analysis tools or information effectively to help the group to develop new insights and solutions and to manage conflict?

　－ Is the facilitator ensuring his or her perceived neutrality by using third parties, group members, and other experts to introduce new analysis tools or information?

　－ Is the facilitator giving the group choices over the analysis tools it uses before asking it to spend substantial time using particular analysis tools?

■ *Conflict engagement:* Is the facilitator intervening to ensure group behaviors result in *productive* conflict (and avoid destructive conflict) during inquiry, advocacy, and decision-making?

- What is the facilitator doing to ensure group members fully share their different expertise, experience or access to information relevant to the task?
- What techniques is the facilitator using to clarify the sources of conflict – discovering the (perceived) differences between group members' views, values or behaviors?
- How is the facilitator ensuring perceived equity within the group during conflict engagement and decision-making?
- Is conflict avoidance – in the form of withdrawal, smoothing or compromising – being highlighted and questioned?
- How are the cost–benefits of conflict being assessed?
- Is the facilitator intervening effectively during destructive conflict?
- Is he or she using role modeling, educating, and calling to account to challenge unproductive behaviors?

## Closing the facilitation event

- ■ What activities will ensure that the group ends the facilitation event with a clear agenda for action and change?
  - Does the *implementation plan* detail the decisions and conclusions reached and outline individuals' responsibility for next steps and follow-up tasks? Are there clear credible short-term tasks and milestones to take their planned changes forward?
  - Does the *stakeholder engagement plan* define how the group will build support and acceptance of change?
- ■ How will the change leader take the recommendations forward?
  - How will you, the change leader, ensure that you understand and learn from the deeper understanding of the business and problem that the group has built during its work (if not present)?
  - What will you, the change leader, do to celebrate the group's success, express appreciation of its work, and recognize its achievements and insights?

## Post-event follow-up

- ■ *Outcome evaluation:* For you, the change leader, the group, the facilitator, and other key stakeholders:
  - What is your evaluation of the *quality* of the solutions and recommen-

dations (the new shared mental model) proposed by the group? Will it resolve the problems identified?

    – Are the solutions and recommendations *shared* by the key people?

■ How is learning from the event being captured?

    – How will individual debriefing take place?

    – What group debriefing will take place to empower the group to learn and create change?

    – What wider organizational issues were highlighted during the facilitation event? Which of those issues will you, as change leader, need to tackle if your change initiative is to succeed?


## Implementation of event outcomes

■ Are the outcomes of the event and the change agenda *clear*?

    – What role will you, the change leader, play in sharing the outcome of the facilitation event?

    – Are organizational stakeholders ready to hear the proposed change plans? What more must you do to increase their readiness for change?

■ Have you ensured that the implementation of change is disciplined?

    – Who is responsible for leading the implementation? Is it the group that developed the solution or others?

    – What support and resources does the implementation group need? Who must participate in follow-up events? What formal follow-up mechanisms and post-event meetings will maintain the momentum of the change implementation?

■ Have you ensured that *accountability* for implementation exists?

    – Who will be monitoring achievement of the implementation plan and the results of change?

    – How (and against what metrics) will individual members of the group be rewarded for their contribution to implementation?

    – How high are the stakes for you, the change leader, the group, and the wider organization? Is there adequate urgency and readiness to support change?

■ In larger organizations, how will the strategic change plan be rolled out to a larger group of key stakeholders?

■ What further events and follow-up will be necessary to overcome the barriers to change that re-emerge when the group working on the solution potentially disperses?

# NOTES

# NOTES

## Introduction

1. Small details have been changed to respect individuals' privacy.

2. *Organizing for successful change management: A McKinsey Global Survey*, July 2006.

3. Engaging people at various levels in the organization is one of the key success factors in transforming organizations; *Organizing for successful change management: A McKinsey Global Survey*, July 2006.

## Section 1: Facilitation – How it works

4. Klimoski, R. and Mohammed, S. (1994) Team mental model: Construct or metaphor? *Journal of Management* **20**: 403–37; Mathieu, J.E., Goodwin, G.F., Heffner, T.S., Salas, E. and Cannon-Bowers, J.A. (2000) The influence of shared mental models on team process and performance, *Journal of Applied Psychology* **85**: 273–83; Mohammed, S. and Dumville, B.C. (2001) Team mental models in a team knowledge framework: expanding theory and measurement across disciplinary boundaries, *Journal of Organizational Behavior* **22**: 89–106.

5. Cannon-Bowers, J.A. and Salas, E. (eds) (1998) *Making Decisions under Stress: Implications for Individual and Team Training*, Washington, D.C.: APA Books.

6. Ibid.

7. Consensus does not necessarily entail full correspondence between intent and interpretation. Agreement between interpretations is perceived, but the interpretations do not have to fit. As Fiol, C.M. (1994, Consensus, diversity and learning in organizations, *Organization Science* **5**(3): 403–20) argues, people may hold different pictures of reality and still agree on the way they frame them.

## Section 2: Planning a facilitation event

8. These roles have been discussed by Gilbert, X., Büchel, B. and Davidson, R. (2007) in *Smarter Execution*, Financial Times/Prentice Hall.

9.  Pia Larsson, *Facilitatorhuset*, pia.larsson@facilitatorhuset.se.

10. Partially adapted from Orsburn, J., Moran, L., Musselwhite, E., and Zenger, J. (1990) *Self-Directed Work Teams*, Business One Irwin.

11. The Deep Dive is a team approach to developing solutions to specific problems or challenges. It is intended to harness the idea-power of everyone on a team in a focused, creative, energetic, fun, and ultimately useful way. A Deep Dive is a combination of brainstorming and prototyping melded together to identify actions to move your company forward. The power of Deep Dives lies in their ability to: concentrate the attention of a management team on a specific design challenge; put the team under considerable time pressure – which has the effect of eliminating unnecessary behaviors that frustrate innovation; create high and explicit expectations of results; encourage ideas outside the norm; encourage the building on the ideas of others; utilize rapid prototyping: and failing often to succeed sooner!

    The Deep Dive was developed by Andy Boynton and Bill Fischer and described in *Virtuoso Teams: Lessons from Teams that Changed the World* (2005) FT/Prentice Hall. In turn the authors gained their inspiration from the process used by design firm IDEO, based in Silicon Valley, ABC News "Nightline: The Deep Dive", July 13, 2003, www.abcnewsstore.com.

## Section 3: Guiding facilitation events

12. Mathieu et al. (2005) *Journal of Organizational Behavior*. The "quality" of "sharedness" of mental models within groups is more important than the "quality" of individual mental models in influencing task and team performance.

13. Hackman, R. (ed.) (1990) *Groups that Work (and Those that Don't): Creating Conditions for Effective Teamwork*, San Francisco: Jossey-Bass.

14. Dr J.C. Lelie *CPF* (Jan). mind@work.

15. Schwarz, R. (2002) *The Skilled Facilitator* (2nd edn), San Francisco: Jossey-Bass, Chapter 5 "Ground Rules for Effective Groups," pp. 96–135.

16. Ibid.

17. Ibid.

18. Kenneth, T. (1992) Overview of conflict and conflict management, *Journal of Organizational Behavior*, p. 269.

19. Adapted from Desivilya, H. and Eizen, D. (2005) Conflict management in work teams: The role of social self-efficacy and group identification, *Journal of Conflict Management*, pp. 183–208.

20. These sample exercises have been used within IMD over a number of

years and have gone through a number of iterations in the process depending on the particular situation. A book by Peter Killing, Tom Malnight and Tracey Keys (2005) *Must Win Battles* also refers to many of these exercises.

# Section 4: Ensuring post-event follow-up and implementation

21. *Organizing for successful change management: A McKinsey Global Survey*, July 2006.

22. Many barriers to implementation are discussed more extensively in Gilbert, X., Büchel, B. and Davidson, R. (2007) *Smarter Execution*, Financial Times/Prentice Hall. Some of the specific steps needed to overcome barriers to implementation are part of what needs to happen to ensure successful execution of strategic initiatives. Ideas for the implementation map in this book are outlined in a more thorough fashion in Gilbert et al.'s book.

23. Source: Büchel, B. (2005) *Charting in New Territory, Perspectives for Managers*, IMD, and Strebel, P. *The Change Pact*, FT, Pitman Publishing.

24. The "Must-Win Battle" concept stems from the book by Killing, P., Malnight, T. and Keys, T. (2005) *Must-Win Battles*, Financial Times/ Prentice Hall.

# Appendix 1: Research findings

25. Mathieu, J.E., Goodwin, G.F., Heffner, T.S., Salas, E. and Cannon-Bowers, J.A. (2000) The influence of shared mental models on team process and performance, *Journal of Applied Psychology* **85**: 273–83; Klimoski, R. and Mohammed, S. (1994). Team mental model: Construct or Metaphor? *Journal of Management* **20**: 403–37; Mohammed, S. and Dumville, B. C. (2001). Team mental models in a team knowledge framework: expanding theory and measurement across disciplinary boundaries, *Journal of Organizational Behavior* **22**: 89–106.

26. Berger, P. and Luckmann, T. (1967) *The Social Construction of Reality*, New York: Doubleday.

27. Mezias, J., Grinyer, P. and Guth, W. (2001) Changing collective cognition: a process model for strategic change, *Long Range Planning*, **24**: 71–95.

28. Berger, P. and Luckmann, T. (1967) *The Social Construction of Reality*, New York: Doubleday.

29. Weick, K. (1995) *Sensemaking in Organizations*, Newbury Park: Sage.

## Appendix 2: Facilitator assessment questionnaire

30. Kolb, J.A. and Rothwell, W.J. (2002) Competencies of small group facilitators: what practitioners view as important, *Journal of European Industrial Training*, pp. 200–3; Nelson, T. and McFadzean, E. (1998) Facilitating problem-solving groups, *Leadership and Organizational Development Journal*, pp. 72–82; McFadzean, E. (2000) Developing and supporting creative problem-solving teams: Part 2 – Facilitator competencies. *Management Decision* **40**: 537–51.

## Appendix 3: Annotated bibliography

31. We would like to acknowledge Don Antunes, Research Fellow at IMD, for contributing to this annotated bibliography.

## Appendix 4: Sample facilitation exercises

32. These sample exercises have been used within IMD over a number of years and have gone through a number of iterations depending on the particular situation. A book by Peter Killing, Tom Malnight and Tracey Keys (2005) *Must-Win Battles: Creating the focus you need to achieve your key business goals* also refers to many of these exercises.

## Appendix 5: Practical issues – location, equipment, and logistics

33. For more details of the Deep Dive process, refer back to the detailed example agenda in Section 2. DeepDive is a trademark of DeepDive Products 2005. All rights reserved. This process has been outlined by IMD faculty Andy Boynton and Bill Fischer. They have also written a book: *Virtuoso Teams: Lessons from Teams that Changed the World* (2005) FT/Prentice Hall.

# INDEX